**To Our Readers:**

INTRODUCING

OTABIND®

INTERNATIONAL

## "The Book That Lies Flat"
### — *User Friendly Binding* —

This title has been bound using state-of-the-art OtaBind® technology.

- The spine is 3-5 times stronger than conventional perfect binding
- The book lies open flat, regardless of the page being read
- The spine floats freely and remains crease-free even with repeated use

We are pleased to be able to bring this new technology to our customers.

**Health Communications, Inc.**

3201 S.W. 15th Street
Deerfield Beach, FL 33442-8190
(305) 360-0909

OTABIND®

INTERNATIONAL

The Netherlands

# AN ACTION PLAN FOR YOUR INNER CHILD
## Parenting Each Other

Laurie Weiss, M.A.

Health Communications, Inc.
Deerfield Beach, Florida

Grateful acknowledgment is made for permission to reprint the following:

"The Greatest Love of All," Copyright © 1977 by C.P.P.-Belwin: words by Linda Creed, music by Michael Masser.

"I Love Myself," © 1991 by Jai-Jo Music, BMI.

Laurie Weiss, M.A.
Littleton, Colorado

Publisher: Health Communications, Inc.
        3201 S.W. 15th Street
        Deerfield Beach, Florida 33442-8190

# ACKNOWLEDGMENTS

I wish I could adequately thank my many teachers and colleagues who have challenged me to think, to work and to create over the years.

Special thanks go to Jean Illsley Clarke, Muriel James, John Bradshaw and the folks at Health Communications for their support and encouragement to keep on writing; I am indebted to the Friends in Recovery, who wrote *The Twelve Steps: A Way Out*, for modeling a workbook for self-help programs.

Preparing the manuscript would have been impossible without the dedicated assistance of many people.

Thank you:

to Valerie Weiler for turning many hours of taped dictation into a workable manuscript, for making sense of my many corrections and for her continuous emotional support throughout the project;

to Madonna Gaudio for reading, editing, re-reading, re-editing, offering valuable suggestions and keeping our office running smoothly at the same time;

to Donna Jara for her able editorial assistance, and for gently and firmly teaching me writing skills through many years of working together;

to Jane Windes who read the manuscript, helped test the material and offered many valuable suggestions;

to my other readers, Elaine Childs-Gowell, Katy Kurtz, Barry Weinhold, Sigrid Farwell and Betty Ching, who offered varied perspectives, wonderful suggestions, and encouragement;

and, finally, to my husband and partner, Jon Weiss, for his incredible support and patience throughout my work on this project, and his countless hours on the computer to prepare the final manuscript.

# CONTENTS

Introduction ................................................................. vii

## Introductory Sessions

Session 1:  Thinking About Parenting Each Other .......................... 1

Session 2:  Creating A Safe Environment For Parenting Each Other .... 17

## Parenting Sessions

Session 3:  Creating Boundaries ................................... 31

Session 4:  I Don't Know What I Want ......................... 41

Session 5:  Learning To Ask ...................................... 51

Session 6:  Holding And Touching ............................ 61

Session 7:  Asking For Closeness ............................... 71

Session 8:  Why? Why? Why? ..................................... 81

Session 9:  Just How Powerful Am I? ........................... 89

Session 10: Making Mistakes Is Okay ........................... 99

Session 11: Negotiation Skills ..................................... 109

Session 12: More About Boundaries ............................ 117

Session 13:   Parenting Your Own Inner Child ................................. 127

Session 14:   Leaving Home ............................................................ 139

Appendix:     How To Organize This Program ................................. 149

References ................................................................................. 217

Bibliography ............................................................................. 219

# INTRODUCTION
## Why Parent Each Other?

Few families are functional enough to provide everything needed to help children grow up to be healthy, functional adults. Growing up in a dysfunctional family can cause serious problems in self-esteem and our ability to relate to others. If you grew up in such a family, you may identify yourself as an Adult Child of an Alcoholic, as an Adult Child of a Dysfunctional Family, as an addict or as a co-dependent. You may be one of millions of people learning to face your problems in a self-help group based on the 12-Step principles of Alcoholics Anonymous and be in a process called recovery.

You may be struggling alone with low self-esteem and relationship problems. You may sometimes feel like a child in a grown-up body, wishing for someone to care for you and teach you how to manage your world. This Inner Child is a part of each of us. This vulnerable, valuable part of us still needs the nurturing we missed when we were children. We all still need some parenting.

People from dysfunctional families have difficulty with relationships. We confuse our needs for grown-up love and companionship with the needs of our Inner Child. The Inner Child longs for the unconditional love and nurturing that are appropriate for chronological children. Adult Children form dysfunctional relationships when we unconsciously try to manipulate other grown-ups into parenting us the way we wish our parents had when we were children.

Adult Children search for the perfect parent to help them grow up and complete developmental tasks. Unfortunately, the only people who seem "right" are those who are much like Mom or Dad and have similar inabilities to meet our needs. With each disappointment we get angry, sometimes end the relationship and often seek another relationship which is equally dysfunctional. The love-disappointment-anger cycle begins again, while the Inner Child's need for parenting remains unfulfilled. The Inner Child grows more and more frustrated and dissatisfied.

The problem is not that the Inner Child needs parenting. The problem is that there are very few ways in which grown-up people can legitimately get parenting from each other.

Mixing parenting into an intimate relationship almost never works. We get confused and don't understand whether we're supposed to be a grown-up partner or a parent to a small child. We live in such a fragmented social system that it is hard to establish ongoing relationships with people of an older generation who might act as surrogate parents. Sometimes parenting is available in a therapy setting. Some forms of parenting are available in self-help recovery groups where people model healthy behavior and support others in learning that behavior. None of these situations, however, provide specific agreements to meet the needs of the Inner Child and help him/her develop skills necessary to grow up healthy.

Parenting is something Adult Children can learn to do for each other. Adult Children often work hard and learn to be effective parents to their biological children. We become frustrated when we try to use these skills to parent ourselves, because we are often unable to give our own Inner Child what we have not received from another person. It is as if our Inner Child is separated from our nurturing grown-up self. We can bridge the separation and get the parenting we need from outside ourselves if we use the resources we have to help each other. By learning to give and receive parenting, we can become healthy parents to our own Inner Children.

**This book presents a program for learning to give and receive appropriate parenting by explicit mutual agreement in the context of a committed support group which will provide safety and help us maintain appropriate boundaries with each other.** We learn to provide each other with the healthy nurturing we've been longing for since we were children. When we get what we need for the Inner Child, we no longer need to try to manipulate others to act as our parents. We become free to learn to have mature relationships with other grown-ups.

In each session we will do centering, writing, nurturing and sharing exercises. There will be supportive activities to do between sessions. There are two introductory sessions. In the first session, we explore and discuss "Thinking About Parenting Each Other." During the second session, we discuss the commitments and agreements each participant is asked to comply with for the duration of the program. In each of the 12 additional sessions, we explore the developmental needs of our Inner Child at a particular age. We will do a series of exercises that allow each participant to have the experience of receiving healthy parenting for significant issues at each stage of development.

*Parenting Each Other* is a 14-session action program designed to be used in support groups. Participants may be drawn from existing 12-Step or other support groups, church groups, treatment centers or simply interested individuals. This program is not designed to be therapy, although a therapist may use it in conjunction with therapy. The program is designed to help you parent your own Inner Child in a healthy and loving manner. When your Inner Child feels secure in your love, your care and your support, you create a strong foundation to help you proceed with your own recovery.

This program may stimulate childhood memories or strong feelings that can best be dealt with in a therapy situation. While a trained professional is not needed to run these groups, a professional consultant may be useful to help you decide if therapy is appropriate.

This book is organized as a workbook; it is designed to help you learn by doing. Each chapter contains the participants' exercises and worksheets for a single session. Instructions for the designated leader (Timekeeper) of each group session are included in the Appendix. The leadership can be rotated so that all members can participate in almost every phase of the program.

**Additional material to help facilitate the organization of *Parenting Each Other* support groups is included in the Appendix: How To Organize This Program. Read this information before you attempt to organize a group.**

Background information is available in the following books:

Weiss, L., & Weiss, J. *Recovery From Co-dependency: It's Never Too Late To Reclaim Your Childhood.* Health Communications, Deerfield Beach, Florida, 1989.

Bradshaw, John. *Homecoming: Reclaiming And Championing Your Inner Child.* Bantam Books, New York, 1990.

Clarke, J. *Self Esteem: A Family Affair.* Winston Press, Minneapolis, Minnesota, 1978.

Clarke, J., & Dawson, C. *Growing Up Again: Parenting Ourselves, Parenting Our Children.* Hazelden/Harper & Row, New York, 1989.

Levin, P. *Becoming The Way We Are: A Transactional Guide To Personal Development.* Health Communications, Deerfield Beach, Florida, 1989.

# Introductory Sessions

## SESSION 1

# THINKING ABOUT PARENTING EACH OTHER

A s a young mother with my first baby, I lived in a time when bottle-feeding was the norm. I chose to breast-feed. My mother and sister both strongly supported bottle-feeding and anxiously questioned me about whether my baby was getting enough to eat. I agonized for several weeks and finally called La Leche League. At the other end of the telephone I found a warm, supportive voice that asked, "Are you breast-feeding?" and affirmed me, "Good for you. Are you having any problems?" By this time I was feeling tearful. The voice offered to send information and encouraged me to call again any time I needed support. Tears of relief ran down my face as I hung up the phone. I wasn't alone. Somebody did care, and somebody could tell me the things I didn't know about how to care for my baby successfully. I was fortunate enough to find someone to parent me when I desperately needed it. With the information and support I received, I was able to relax and learn to be a good Mom.

## WHAT IS HEALTHY PARENTING?

Parenting is providing someone with something they need to live and grow that they can't yet give themselves. When parenting is successful, the

1

receiver incorporates the parenting as part of herself and no longer needs it from an outside source. It takes children years to learn to parent themselves in a healthy manner. Grown-ups, however, can often incorporate healthy parenting very quickly. Jean Illsley Clarke and Connie Dawson (*Growing Up Again: Parenting Ourselves, Parenting Our Children*) describe the elements of healthy parenting as nurture and structure. Nurture provides the loving support and the affirmation of their being that children need. Nurture provides the mirroring that says, "I know you're here. I'm glad you're alive. Hurray for you!" Structure helps children learn limits, skills and appropriate rules for living successfully. Children of different ages need structure and nurture in different forms. Healthy parenting involves being aware of what's needed and providing it in a way that encourages the growth of a child.

Adults, too, need caring and loving responses, information, limits and support. This parenting is often provided by relatives, friends, teachers and mentors who feel comfortable about themselves and offer support spontaneously or in response to requests. Healthy parenting usually results in a grown-up feeling affirmed, empowered and relieved. My attempts to breast-feed were affirmed by my La Leche phone call. The information empowered me and I felt relief from my feelings of fear, loneliness and uncertainty.

Healthy parenting for grownups is available in many forms.

• A businesswomen's organization introduces new entrepreneurs to successful business owners who offer to provide support and information that will enable the less experienced women to be successful.

• Ralph coaches a friend about how to prepare for a job interview.

• Anna's AA sponsor calls to encourage her to continue working on her fourth step.

• Lisa's sister went with her to the doctor when she was going to learn about a procedure that she was afraid of. Her sister provided reassurance and a second set of ears to listen to the information and ask questions until they were both sure they understood.

• When Jim's Dad died, a friend came and made travel arrangements for Jim to go to the funeral, helped him pack and held him as he wept.

## Worksheet #1: Healthy Parenting For Grown-ups

List at least three people who have provided healthy parenting for you in your grown-up life. Using a separate sheet of paper answer the following questions about each person:

1. Name: _____

2. What did they do? _____

3. When did they do this? _____

4. How did you feel before they did this? _____

5. How did you feel afterwards? _____

6. What changes did you make because of this experience? _____

_____

### SHARING EXERCISE

Complete Worksheet #1. Follow the Timekeeper's instructions and share with the group what you have written. Give your undivided attention to others when they are sharing. Do not interrupt or attempt to "fix" another person. If you choose not to share, say, "I pass" when it is your turn. Keep anything you learn about others confidential.

## Adult Children Need Parenting

No parents are perfect; therefore, no adult ever got everything s/he needed as a child. All grown-ups need supplemental parenting. We often use a variety of unclear and manipulative methods in our attempts to get the parenting we need.

Some adults substitute authority figures (bosses, teachers, spouses) for parents and then continue to have difficulty with them.

Beverly has a love/hate relationship with her boss. When her boss provides warm and nurturing support, Beverly loves her. When her boss expects Beverly to be responsible and operate without frequent contact, Beverly hates her and re-experiences the abandonment she felt as a child growing up in a dysfunctional family.

Some Adult Children choose abusive relationships, bond with dysfunctional people and have great difficulty in separating. Others choose distancing relationships and then blame their partners for lack of appropriate closeness.

Sherry's husband continually berated her for imagined inadequacies. As she had done while growing up, she assumed he was correct, tried to do better and felt terrible about herself. She was extremely unhappy with her husband, yet she kept saying to herself, "I love him too much to get a divorce."

Substance abusers may become so dysfunctional that someone is forced to step in and take a parent or caretaker role.

Jim gets so drunk that he passes out and soils himself. He wakes up the next morning unaware that his wife cleaned him up and put him to bed.

Even adults who grew up in relatively healthy families still need parenting. Parents may be temporarily unavailable due to circumstances in their own lives.

Andy's parents were in an automobile accident when he was two. Although they survived, the abrupt separation that lasted for months caused significant damage to his belief that the world was trustworthy and secure. He turned to alcohol to soothe his fears and repeatedly felt abandoned and betrayed by friends who grew tired of his drunken, irresponsible behavior.

These confused attempts to get parenting prove over and over again that parents are unreliable. The Inner Child becomes certain they will never be able to find the parenting she or he longs for.

## Worksheet #2: Authorities As Parents

(1) What do you wish that your mother, father or other caretakers had done differently when you were a child? _____

_____

(2) How are you still looking for what they didn't give you? _____

_____

(3) List three to five authority figures in your life currently:

1. _____
2. _____
3. _____
4. _____
5. _____

(4) How do you feel when you are with each person? Are you content? Competitive? Are you resentful, angry, scared, ashamed? Answer the question for each person listed above.

1. _____
2. _____
3. _____
4. _____
5. _____

(5) What have you learned by answering these questions? _____

_____

**SHARING EXERCISE**

Complete Worksheet #2. Follow the Timekeeper's instructions and share your answers in your group.

### *"I Can Do It Myself!"*

This refrain of all Adult Children usually means "I had to do it myself when I was a child" or "I was hurt or shamed if I asked for the help or nurturing I needed." Although Adult Children may be able to parent others effectively some of the time, we are usually very hard on ourselves. We parent others by following instructions in books and from courses, often ignoring our own needs. We use an Inner Parent to parent ourselves with self-talk we learned by listening to the grown-ups who cared for us when we were children. Although some of the self-talk is positive and healthy, much of it is negative and destructive, often including esteem-destroying messages like these: "You're stupid. You should have known that. You should be strong. You shouldn't have to ask for help. You don't deserve it. What makes you think you have any rights?"

If you were abused or neglected in your family-of-origin, you probably abuse or neglect yourself. If you were treated harshly or rigidly or were abandoned to your own devices, you probably use your Inner Parent to parent yourself the same way. Although you may take thoughtful steps to avoid parenting others the way you were parented, you may have great difficulty using that information to parent yourself in a loving way.

There are many techniques to help you replace those negative statements you repeat to yourself. Using affirmations, participating in recovery programs and listening to appropriate coaching are all useful. The most effective way to replace those critical voices with loving and appropriate messages is to let yourself be in a vulnerable position, with your Inner Child available. Then, in a safe environment, have someone else give healthy messages directly to your Inner Child. These messages provide alternatives for the negative ones you learned as a child and give you something positive to say to yourself.

## Worksheet #3: Your Inner Parent

Answer these questions:

1. What do you say to yourself when you make a mistake? _____

_____

2. What do you say to yourself when you have more things to do than time to do

    them in? _____

_____

3. What do you say to yourself when you are faced with a complex task you've never done before and aren't sure how to accomplish? _____

_____

4. What do you say to yourself when you are in a meeting and need to go to the bathroom? _____

_____

5. Does your Inner Parent treat your Inner Child with love? _____

_____

6. Does your Inner Parent treat your Inner Child with respect? _____

_____

7. Does your Inner Parent set appropriate limits with your Inner Child? _____

_____

## SHARING EXERCISE

Complete Worksheet #3. Follow the Timekeeper's instructions and share your answers in your group.

### Why Parent Each Other?

Adult Children have an underlying belief in their own unworthiness, and yet they can easily see the strength and beauty in others. In order to appreciate ourselves, we need to be appreciated by someone else. If we missed the loving responsiveness (mirroring) we needed when we were tiny infants, we may learn to feel ashamed of the part of ourselves that wants and needs nurturing (our own Inner Child). Each time we try to nurture that Inner Child we meet resistance that may take a very long time to overcome. Being nurtured by someone who accepts our Inner Child without qualification can be an extremely powerful experience and break through years of painstaking struggle.

Often when Adult Children parent others, we feel sad and resentful because we are giving away the very thing that our own Inner Child needs so desperately. When we parent each other by agreement and design instead of by manipulation and exploitation, we do get back what we give away.

## Worksheet #4: Parenting Others

Whom do you parent now? (Circle the answer.)

Children      Spouse or significant other      Your parents      Friends

Co-workers     Others _____

List one or two people you currently parent and answer these questions about each person:

Person #1 _____

Person #2 _____

1. Does this person appreciate your efforts? _____

2. Do you feel as if you're doing a good job? _____

3. What kind of results do you get? _____

4. How do you feel about parenting them? _____

5. Do you resent giving away what your Inner Child wants and needs?

_____

6. Do you wish that they would take care of *your* Inner Child? _____

_____

### SHARING EXERCISE

Complete Worksheet #4. When you are done, follow the Timekeeper's instructions and share with other members of your group your answers about one of the people you parent.

### Parenting Without Exploitation

To exploit is to use for one's own benefit, often unfairly. In dysfunctional families, adults may use children to meet their own needs, often without regard for the needs of the children. Children learn to cooperate in their own exploitation to ensure their survival or continued care. They cooperate by: not expressing their own needs in order to avoid bothering their parents, taking care of the needs of others in order to help their parents, and engaging in behavior that calls attention to themselves and away from other problems in the family.

Children need parents to care for them and will do almost anything to avoid being abandoned. The behaviors we learn as children continue into adulthood, and we allow ourselves to be exploited because of old habits and continuing fear. When parenting each other we need to create carefully a safe and supportive environment in which no individual is encouraged or permitted to sacrifice himself or herself for the benefit of others.

A safe environment will be created cooperatively by having all of us agree to clear rules and expectations. We will explain all activities in advance and give each person an opportunity to choose their level of participation. We will strive to create a consistently safe environment where we can talk about our experiences and respond appropriately to each other's needs and feelings. We will build trust gradually by first taking small risks and observing the results. When the results are favorable, we can gradually increase our level of risk. Your Inner Child does not need to be hurt again!

There is much confusion in our culture between nurturing and sexuality. We will take special care to avoid the risk of sexual exploitation. We will ask each participant to agree not to have any kind of sexual contact with any other participant in the program for the duration of the program and for six months thereafter. (This rule will not apply to people who are in a committed sexual relationship before the start of the program.)

## Worksheet #5:  Creating Safety

What structures and boundaries help your Inner Child feel safe? Mark your preference on each scale.

### TIME

| *Starting exactly on time* | | | | *Starting whenever we feel like it* | | |
|:---:|:---:|:---:|:---:|:---:|:---:|:---:|
| 1 | 2 | 3 | 4 | 5 | 6 | 7 |
| Strongly favor | Favor | Slightly favor | Neutral | Slightly favor | Favor | Strongly favor |

### PLACE

| *Always meeting in the same room* | | | | *Meeting in different rooms* | | |
|:---:|:---:|:---:|:---:|:---:|:---:|:---:|
| 1 | 2 | 3 | 4 | 5 | 6 | 7 |
| Strongly favor | Favor | Slightly favor | Neutral | Slightly favor | Favor | Strongly favor |

### PEOPLE

| *Always the same people* (closed membership) | | | | *New people each time* (open membership) | | |
|:---:|:---:|:---:|:---:|:---:|:---:|:---:|
| 1 | 2 | 3 | 4 | 5 | 6 | 7 |
| Strongly favor | Favor | Slightly favor | Neutral | Slightly favor | Favor | Strongly favor |

## RESPONSIVENESS

*People always respond and
validate each other*                                    *People don't respond*

| 1 | 2 | 3 | 4 | 5 | 6 | 7 |
|---|---|---|---|---|---|---|
| Strongly favor | Favor | Slightly favor | Neutral | Slightly favor | Favor | Strongly favor |

## AGREEMENTS

*All agreements kept*                                    *No agreements kept*

| 1 | 2 | 3 | 4 | 5 | 6 | 7 |
|---|---|---|---|---|---|---|
| Strongly favor | Favor | Slightly favor | Neutral | Slightly favor | Favor | Strongly favor |

## TRUTH

*People tell the truth
as they experience it*                              *People say what they think
other people want to hear*

| 1 | 2 | 3 | 4 | 5 | 6 | 7 |
|---|---|---|---|---|---|---|
| Strongly favor | Favor | Slightly favor | Neutral | Slightly favor | Favor | Strongly favor |

## SHARING EXERCISE

Complete Worksheet #5. When you are done, follow the Timekeeper's instructions and discuss your responses and your reasons for them in your small group. First, have each person discuss time, then place, etc.

### Nurturing Exchange

Parenting each other means that we each give parenting and we each receive parenting. Most Adult Children find it easier to nurture another than to receive nurturing. However, some Adult Children prefer the receiver position. We may believe that "others should take care of me" and may need to learn to give. Most of us experience problems balancing giving and receiving.

# Worksheet #6:  Giving And Receiving

Learning to receive is an essential element of this program.

Do you find it easier to give or receive? _____
Some reasons Adult Children give for being uncomfortable receiving nurturing include the following:

1. If I open myself to nurturing, I'll never get enough.
2. I don't trust anybody to nurture me.

3. If I accept nurturing from you, I may come to trust you; then I'll be betrayed again.
4. I'll owe something if I accept nurturing.
5. If I accept nurturing, I might show emotion. That will prove that I'm weak; then someone could take advantage of me.
6. I'm bad and selfish if I want anything for myself.
7. The other person doesn't really want to nurture me.
8. I don't know how.
9. I don't want to give away what I need for myself.
10. I have nothing to give.
11. I don't think anyone would accept nurturing from me.
12. I'll be rejected.
13. I'm trying to stop being co-dependent.

Which of these statements seems true to you? (Circle them.)

Are there other reasons why you find it difficult to give or receive? _____

---

Who are the special people you allow to nurture you? What makes them special? _____

## SHARING EXERCISE

Complete Worksheet #6. When you're done, follow the Timekeeper's instructions and share your answers with the group.

### Introduction: Accepting Compliments

As we gradually expose our vulnerable Inner Children to each other, we can learn to trust a little bit at a time. The following exercise is slightly more risky than the others we've done. It invites you to expose yourself directly to another in order to practice receiving nurturing. It's okay to pass and not participate. If you choose this alternative, ask whether you may observe two people who are participating.

## EXERCISE: ACCEPTING COMPLIMENTS

Think of a compliment you turned down recently. (You turn down compliments by saying things like, "Anyone can do that" or "This old thing?" or "If you really knew me, you wouldn't say that.")

Choose a partner. Tell your partner the compliment you turned down, repeating as closely as possible the exact words used. It is the partner's job to repeat the compliment to you three times.

The first time your partner gives you the compliment, turn it down the way you did originally.

The second time your partner repeats the compliment to you, take a deep breath, feel the compliment and say, "Thank you."

The third time your partner repeats the compliment to you, say thank you and embellish the compliment. You embellish the compliment by saying something additional about it. For example, if someone says to you, "The color you're wearing looks well on you," say, "Thank you very much. It's one of my favorite colors." If someone comments on the changes you've made in how you treat other people, say, "Thank you very much. I've been working really hard to make those changes."

After you've completed this exercise, switch roles with your partner and repeat the exercise so your partner has the opportunity to practice accepting a compliment that s/he had turned down before. In your small group share how you felt during each phase of giving and receiving your compliments.

## What To Expect

As you participate in this program, your Inner Child will take a more active role in your life. The various exercises may assist you in remembering childhood experiences, and you may have strong feelings of fear, anger and sadness that weren't safe for you to express or feel when you were a child growing up in a dysfunctional family. After those feelings are released, you may experience joy, happiness, satisfaction and relief as your Inner Child learns that the world is a safe place, that your needs and feelings count and that you are competent to make an impact on your environment and get a healthy response.

Assimilating these experiences will enable you to successfully self-parent your own Inner Child in some areas, as well as feel much more comfortable in parenting others, especially your own children. It will also increase your skills in the areas listed on this questionnaire.

Before the next session, circle the number on the following questionnaire which represents your level of competence in each area. Using a different color of ink, circle the level of competence you would like to reach in each area. Remember to be realistic.

# SELF-ASSESSMENT QUESTIONNAIRE

| | Never | Seldom | Sometimes | Often | Always |
|---|---|---|---|---|---|

1. I know when my body needs something (food, air, water, rest, etc.).  1 2 3 4 5 6 7 8 9 10

2. I am effective about making sure my environment supports my physical needs.  1 2 3 4 5 6 7 8 9 10

3. I know when I need strokes.  1 2 3 4 5 6 7 8 9 10

4. I am comfortable in new situations.  1 2 3 4 5 6 7 8 9 10

5. I can try out new things without getting in trouble or hurting myself.  1 2 3 4 5 6 7 8 9 10

6. I am comfortable selecting what I like and don't like in new situations.  1 2 3 4 5 6 7 8 9 10

7. I can enjoy myself by exploring something new.  1 2 3 4 5 6 7 8 9 10

8. I feel independent and autonomous.  1 2 3 4 5 6 7 8 9 10

9. When I make decisions, I count myself and others equally.  1 2 3 4 5 6 7 8 9 10

10. I am comfortable sharing my ideas and opinions with others who have ideas of their own, even if their ideas differ from mine.  1 2 3 4 5 6 7 8 9 10

11. I am comfortable about the ways in which I am different from others.  1 2 3 4 5 6 7 8 9 10

12. I am comfortable about the ways in which I am similar to others.  1 2 3 4 5 6 7 8 9 10

13. I am able to be vocal and stubborn in opposing things I think are destructive.  1 2 3 4 5 6 7 8 9 10

14. I am comfortable asking questions when I don't understand or want to know something.  1 2 3 4 5 6 7 8 9 10

15. I can recognize and acknowledge other people's feelings.  1 2 3 4 5 6 7 8 9 10

| | Never | Seldom | Sometimes | Often | Always |
|---|---|---|---|---|---|
| 16. I have the ability to find out what others feel when I don't know. | 1  2 | 3  4 | 5  6  7 | 8 | 9  10 |
| 17. I can confront others when I see problems in what they are doing, saying or feeling. | 1  2 | 3  4 | 5  6  7 | 8 | 9  10 |
| 18. I can tell when to give up on something that isn't working. | 1  2 | 3  4 | 5  6  7 | 8 | 9  10 |
| 19. I am willing to feel sadness and grief when I have to let go of something that was important to me. | 1  2 | 3  4 | 5  6  7 | 8 | 9  10 |
| 20. I am comfortable learning how to do new things that I didn't know how to do before. | 1  2 | 3  4 | 5  6  7 | 8 | 9  10 |
| 21. I do things as well as they need to be done. | 1  2 | 3  4 | 5  6  7 | 8 | 9  10 |
| 22. I finish things that need to be finished. | 1  2 | 3  4 | 5  6  7 | 8 | 9  10 |
| 23. I can recognize and communicate the reasons for my values and beliefs. | 1  2 | 3  4 | 5  6  7 | 8 | 9  10 |
| 24. I can recognize and understand that others have different reasons for their values and beliefs. | 1  2 | 3  4 | 5  6  7 | 8 | 9  10 |
| 25. I am comfortable negotiating openly with others to satisfy our needs and wants. | 1  2 | 3  4 | 5  6  7 | 8 | 9  10 |
| 26. I recognize and am comfortable with the fact that I am connected to other people. | 1  2 | 3  4 | 5  6  7 | 8 | 9  10 |
| 27. I can be interdependent with others without sacrificing my own autonomy. | 1  2 | 3  4 | 5  6  7 | 8 | 9  10 |

(From *Recovery From Co-Dependency: It's Never Too Late To Reclaim Your Childhood* by Laurie Weiss and Jonathan B. Weiss.)

People raised in healthy families, and people who are well along in recovery, often circle items at level 8 or above. You are your own best judge of the level of improvement you would like to see. We will use this questionnaire throughout the program as we do specific exercises to increase your level of competence in each area.

*BRING THE COMPLETED QUESTIONNAIRE WITH YOU TO EVERY SESSION.*

## Between Sessions

Read the Introduction and Chapters 1 and 2 in *Recovery From Co-Dependency: It's Never Too Late To Reclaim Your Childhood.* Notice where you get parenting. Notice where you wish you could get parenting.

Begin a journal where you can record any thoughts that are stimulated by your participation in this program. This is for your use only. You don't have to write in sentences, spell correctly or use punctuation. Just write your thoughts.

## Closing Song

Form a circle, join hands and sing together the "unofficial theme song" of the Adult Children's movement, "The Greatest Love of All." The words are on page 15.

## The Greatest Love Of All

I believe the children are our future.
Teach them well and let them lead the way.
Show them all the beauty they possess inside.
Give them a sense of pride to make it easier.
Let the children's laughter remind us how we used to be.

Everybody's searching for a hero.
People need someone to look up to.
I never found anyone who fulfilled my need.
A lonely place to be, so I learned to depend on me.

I decided long ago never to walk in anyone's shadow.
If I fail, if I succeed, at least I'll live as I believe.
No matter what they take from me, they can't take away my dignity.

Because the greatest love of all was happening to me.
I found the greatest love of all inside of me.
The greatest love of all is easy to achieve.
Learning to love yourself is the greatest love of all.

I believe the children are our future.
Teach them well and let them lead the way.
Show them all the beauty they possess inside.
Give them a sense of pride to make it easier.
Let the children's laughter remind us how we used to be.

I decided long ago never to walk in anyone's shadow.
If I fail, if I succeed, at least I'll live as I believe.
No matter what they take from me, they can't take away my dignity.

Because the greatest love of all was happening to me.
I found the greatest love of all inside of me.
The greatest love of all is easy to achieve.
Learning to love yourself is the greatest love of all.

And if by chance that special place
That you've been dreaming of
Leads you to a lonely place
Find your strength in love.

---

# SESSION 2

# CREATING A SAFE ENVIRONMENT FOR PARENTING EACH OTHER

## MAKING A COMMITMENT TO THE PROCESS

Change is difficult for Adult Children. We know we need to do it, but a part of us holds us back. We listen to conflicting inner voices. A grown-up part responds to current reality, takes in information, sorts it, makes predictions about what will happen if the information is used and says, "Go ahead." Our Inner Parent restates the rules we learned from our caretakers as well as the new, sometimes conflicting rules we have decided to follow during our recovery process. This Inner Parent may urge us on toward recovery or attempt to stop us. The voice of the Inner Child conveys hope, fear and caution.

### Worksheet #7: Your Inner Voices

Record some of the statements your inner voices are making about your participation in the program.

My Inner Child says:

_____

_____

My Inner Parent says:

_____

_____

My Adult says:

_____

_____

SHARING EXERCISE

Follow the Timekeeper's instructions and share these statements with others in your small group.

## The Power Of Survival Decisions

Your Inner Child decided long ago what behavior was necessary to get the attention you needed from the folks who took care of you. If you lived in a relatively healthy environment, the things you needed to do enhanced your own natural growth and development toward maturity. The more restrictive, neglectful or abusive your environment became, the more likely that your survival depended on doing things that limited your movement toward maturity and health.

Your Inner Child figured out what worked in that long ago environment and is understandably reluctant to change anything that did work, even though your environment has changed. After all, the Inner Child's strategy got you through the original trauma, helped you survive and got you where you are today. No wonder it is reluctant to "mess with success" by changing what worked in the past.

While children are vulnerable, imperfect, dependent and immature (*Facing Co-dependence,* Pia Mellody, et al.), they are also tenacious, tough and creative. As babies, we have few available resources. We can barely move around without help. We certainly can't take care of ourselves, except by doing or not doing things in order to please our caretakers, so this is what we learn to do. Despite our immaturity and imperfection, we are astute observers of the world we live in. We quickly learn about cause and effect: we notice what we do that brings us comfort and what we do that brings us pain. While still too young to distinguish ourselves clearly from our caretakers, we learn to do things like smiling, if smiling brings the increased comfort of being held in another's arms and fed. We learn to stop crying, if crying brings increased pain because we're spanked or shaken instead of comforted when we express our distress.

As babies the fact that we don't have words to think with doesn't mean we aren't thinking and making decisions about all these things we're learning. We think with our feelings and make our decisions viscerally, on the basis of "gut-level" information. It is as if we think with our whole bodies, not just our brains, and therefore our early memories and decisions may be held in our bodies even more deeply than they are held in our minds. We may not have conscious awareness of these early decisions, but they nevertheless continue to have a profound influence on our lives.

Many of the wordless, gut-level decisions we make as tiny children are designed to ensure our survival. If we'd had words to express these important decisions, they might sound like this: "From now on, I won't do anything that will get me hurt. From now on, I won't trust anyone. From now on, I'll be good."

Once we've made a survival decision, we "know" in our bodies that we need to honor it. Our Inner Child "knows," on a gut level, that we have survived only because we have done exactly what we have done, in exactly the way we did it. We therefore experience fear, even terror, when we attempt to change things we've been doing for our whole lives. If we try to do something else, the Inner Child may take control of our bodies and cause us to feel anxious and uncomfortable. If the change strongly violates a survival decision, we might even sweat, panic or throw up.

## Problems With Survival Decisions

The survival decisions we made as small children were good and healthy decisions for us, given our limited resources at the time we made them. Unfortunately, these decisions caused us to screen out new information that perhaps would have let us try new approaches to the world. From the child's perspective *we don't want to do anything* that will compromise our safety or security. When we try to change, our Inner Child often stops us with the cry, "It's not safe, be careful! I'm uncomfortable. I don't want to! Let me outta here!" If our Inner Child is less assertive, we may protect ourselves by losing interest, falling asleep or diverting our attention to our addictions and compulsions.

When we get a little older we become more sophisticated in maneuvering within our families to get the maximum available nurturing. We figure out what we need to do in order to get attention from our biological parents, siblings, grandparents, other relatives or babysitters. We avoid the pain that may come with doing the wrong thing in our family. When we do experience pain from neglect or abuse, we may learn to shut off all feelings or do something that distracts us from the pain.

As we get older, we may find other ways of coping with the pain of not getting parenting which supports our growth. We may learn to use alcohol, drugs, food, work, sex, physical illness, achievement, excitement and many other behaviors that can become addictive or compulsive, to divert our attention from our Inner Child's needs and pain. At the same time, our Inner Child still hopes for nurturing and looks for anyone who might be able to provide it.

Often we get familiar criticism instead of nurturing. We may try to get nurturing by getting into situations where others feel compelled to take care of us. If we do receive the nurturing we've longed for, we may find it hard to accept because we don't recognize or trust it. We feel ambivalent about receiving any parenting. We feel resentful when we are not treated as responsible, mature adults, while at the same time the Inner Child is desperately seeking what he or she never had. This is a highly unsatisfactory and confusing situation, yet it continues because going against those old gut-level decisions feels even worse.

## Worksheet #8: Early Decisions

Here are some situations designed to help you identify the decisions you made as a child. If you grew up with extreme abuse or neglect, it may be difficult for you to complete some of the responses. If so, just complete as many of the situations as you can.

(1) When I was a child, in order to get positive attention from my caretakers I had to (examples: take care of my siblings, get good grades, etc.):

_____

_____

(2) When I was a child, in order to get positive attention from my caretakers, I had to avoid (examples: asking for what I wanted, being noisy, interrupting adults):

_____

_____

(3) When I was a child, in order to avoid negative attention from my caretakers, I had to (examples: be very quiet, listen to criticism, etc.):

_____

_____

(4) When I was a child, in order to avoid negative attention from my caretakers, I had to stop myself from (examples: talking back, doing what I wanted to do, etc.):

_____

_____

(5) Which of the things you learned as a child (to get positive attention or avoid negative attention) do you still do in your current life? _____

_____

(6) To avoid pain or to get the attention I needed, I learned to use: drugs
alcohol      food      work      sex      achievement      excitement

physical  illness

other _____.

(Circle the answers that apply or fill in your own.)

Remember that when you use one of these behaviors compulsively, it's probably because your Inner Child is wishing for the parenting that would have been appropriate when you were small.

SHARING EXERCISE

Follow the Timekeeper's directions and share your responses in your small group.

## The Parenting Sessions

Each session will begin with a *Sharing Exercise* to help participants make the transition from getting to the meeting to being in the meeting. Each person will briefly share what they feel like saying about anything at all, then give the next person a chance to share. This time is for sharing anything that is important at the moment. You can talk about how the traffic was on the way to the session, important things you've learned in a previous session or activities you have done between sessions. You will do several rounds of sharing, responding nonverbally to each speaker until the personal business that might distract you from participation in the session has been expressed.

The next exercise in each session will ask you to focus on some aspect of your everyday life. You will fill in a *Worksheet* and then discuss your answers with other members of your small group.

Next is a *Centering Ritual.* The members of your entire group will stand in a circle, hold hands and sing together "The Greatest Love of All," which will help remind you of the purpose of parenting each other: learning to love yourself. This song will help you focus your attention within yourself to prepare for a visualization experience.

During the *Visualization* segment, you will be asked to imagine stepping into the life of a child growing up in a healthy family and experience what it is like to be parented in a healthy way. After this exercise, you'll have the opportunity to write in your journal about your experience and then discuss the exercise with other members of your small group.

The next exercise is a *Nurturing Exchange* in which you take turns actually parenting each other, as if one of you is a small child and the other a healthy parent. Before you participate in this exercise, you will have a chance to discuss and clear any reservations you may have about participation.

After the first *Nurturing Exchange* you will write about your experience and then share what you have written with your partner. After a brief break you will choose a new partner and repeat the exchange, this time taking the opposite role.

When the sharing after that exchange is complete, the group leader will review the necessary *Preparation For The Next Session* and will complete any other administrative details.

The session will close with another song.

There will be a list of many optional activities to do *Between Sessions,* to help you integrate what you've learned and to extend your learning. These activities are all optional. If you choose to do them, don't attempt to do all of them; there are too many. Choose the ones that most appeal to you.

This is a powerful program. You can expect an emotional response to many of the activities. You may find yourself dreaming differently. You may start thinking a lot about what happened to you when you were a child. You may even experience flashbacks, memories or fragments of memories of long-forgotten events, sometimes accompanied by strong emotions. You will probably think about what you need in your life now, and about how to parent your own children more effectively.

Write about your experiences in your workbook. You may also want to bring along a small notebook for added writing space. Keeping a record will enhance your learning and also allow you to review your progress long after you've completed the program. If you are in therapy, you may want to discuss your notes with your therapist.

Your workbook is for you alone. When you write, don't worry about spelling, punctuation, spacing or editing. Record your thoughts and impressions as they occur. There is no correct way to do this.

Your main responsibilities will be:

- Gathering your materials.
- Showing up on time.

- Participating.
- Keeping your commitments and agreements.
- Doing your homework and homeplay.
- Recording what you learn.
- Sharing with other group members.
- Being responsible for asking others for any assistance you may need.

## Commitment To The Program

For you to get the benefits offered by this program and to protect yourself and others from potential hurt, it's important that all participants in the program commit to certain basic agreements. Making these commitments to yourself will help you stick with this program even at those times when your Inner Child is frightened or your Inner Parent repeats voices from the past, trying to divert you from your course.

Please read the following statements of commitment and discuss them with your group. Follow the Timekeeper's instructions.

I _____ know I needed more parenting than my parents had available for me. This need for nurturing has influenced my life and caused my Inner Child to seek parenting inappropriately from friends, lovers, spouses, bosses and even my own children. My creative Inner Child has begged, pleaded, cajoled, manipulated, played games, gotten sick or used chemicals in an attempt to get what I think I need. She or he has never quite understood that the world is different now, that the ways she or he used to get even a little nurturing in my family-of-origin are no longer necessary. I am now an adult. I can create my own safety. I no longer need the charade to try to get nurturing. (These methods never did work very well, anyhow.)

I _____ acknowledge that although my parents did the best they could, they were unable to supply me with many of the important responses I needed to become a healthy adult.

I _____ commit to learning to become a healthy parent to my own Inner Child; I commit to exchanging nurturing with others in the program so we may each learn to nurture the Inner Child within each of us.

When you are ready to make this commitment, please complete and sign your copy.

_____                    _____
(Signature)                                                                      (Date)

## Agreements For Creating Safety, Trust And Consistency

Children living in dysfunctional families learn not to trust others. They feel insecure and unsafe because the environment is often chaotic, and agreements are not kept or are never made in the first place. In order to create an environment where your Inner Child experiences safety, we need to be as consistent as we can. Understanding and keeping these agreements will gradually make it safe for your Inner Child to experience the nurturing that he or she needs. Although it would be nice to be 100 percent certain of safety, that isn't the way the world works. At our best, we're imperfect; that's why the first agreement is:

1. *When I participate in this program, I will do my best to keep the following agreements.*

Your best will probably not be 100 percent perfect, and that's okay. In your small group, discuss these agreements one at a time. As you agree to honor each one, initial it. After you've completed the discussion, sign the agreements list on page 29.

2. *I will be responsive to others.*

Being responsive means acknowledging when someone else is communicating. Look at people when they speak. Listen to what they say. Respond nonverbally by nodding and/or letting your feelings show. Practice active listening.

Active listening is the process of repeating back to someone the essence of what they've said to you. For example, if someone tells a long, involved story about how they didn't know what to do in a given situation, you might say back to them, "It sounds as if you were confused," or "I understand how confusing that must have been for you." For additional information about active listening, read Thomas Gordon's *Parent Effectiveness Training.*

If someone is experiencing strong emotions, stay with them. Don't abandon them by looking away or retreating to your own discomfort. Acknowledge them by saying, "I can see that you're upset (scared, angry, crying, whatever)." Offer support by asking, "Would you like me to hold your hand? Put my arm around your shoulders? Hug you?" You can also reassure them by saying, "This is a safe place to feel feelings; I'll stay with you." It's okay to go on with your discussion as long as the person experiencing the feelings is receiving support and not being ignored.

If someone is doing something that causes a problem for you, first, describe the behavior you find distressing, then ask them to change it by doing something else instead. For example, Jim could say to Sarah, "You started to tell me your own story when I was telling you what happened yesterday. Next time, please wait until I finish before you tell me what you did." In your discussion group, discuss possible responses to the following situations:

- Someone talks about his or her father promising to come to a school program and not showing up.
- Someone gives you advice you don't want.
- Someone talks about feeling shamed by what they have just revealed to you in the group.

3. *I will tell the truth about my own experiences.*

This is easy to do when we're talking about something that happened outside the meeting; however, it's often difficult to share uncomfortable feelings as they occur. Most of us grow up in dysfunctional families in which certain feelings are not permitted. If you feel angry, frightened or sad, it's important to acknowledge those feelings when you are talking to others. It isn't necessary to do anything about them in this setting, just acknowledge them.

You can acknowledge your feelings by saying, "I feel (mad, glad, sad, scared) when (I/you) (say, think, do) that."

4. *I will keep confidential anything I learn about others in this program.*

It's fine to tell other people what you have done or learned about yourself in the program; however, you don't have the right to share information about other people without their permission. You wouldn't want to be talked about outside the program. This agreement makes it safe for everyone to talk about experiences they don't want shared outside the program.

5. *I will use the healthy part of myself to nurture others during the program.*
*If I have doubts or questions, I will get clarification before proceeding.*

Even if you're unable to nurture your own Inner Child, there's a part of you that believes other people deserve love and respect. There will be exercises to help you use this part of you when it is time to nurture someone else. If you don't feel you can provide a particular response, pretending won't help anybody. It's all right to have doubts. You can say, "This isn't true for me now, but I believe it can be true for you." The person you are nurturing will just get confused if you try to pretend.

You may experience a strong drive to parent others the way you were parented. Therefore you need to remain conscious of what you say and do. *It is extremely important that you don't use criticism, sarcasm, mixed or hidden messages or put-downs when communicating with other group members.*

Humor at the expense of another can be very damaging. Almost everyone learns to cover pain with laughter. If someone laughingly describes something painful, negative or destructive about themselves or others, don't laugh. Instead, say, "That doesn't seem funny to me," or "That sounds like it really hurts."

6. *I will nurture in the ways suggested by the program and will discuss deviations from the instructions with at least three other people before deciding what to do.*

If you have a strong reaction to what you're being asked to do, there is a reason for it. Based on your past experience, you may believe that what you're being asked to do is wrong or stupid, or that it may cause someone harm. You might fear a strong emotional response if you follow through on the instructions, particularly if you are being asked to give someone else something that you have longed for. Just discussing these activities may awaken long-buried memories of childhood experiences. You may feel unable to do the nurturing task effectively.

Discuss your response and the reasons for it with members of your group and then discuss your options. You may decide not to participate or to modify what you're doing. The decision is yours. The other members of your group can reorganize and figure out how to make sure each person receives the suggested nurturing experience, even if you don't participate.

7. *I will accept the nurturing that is offered in the program. If at any time I do not wish to do so, I will discuss this with at least three other members of the program and then make my own decision.*

It's sometimes difficult to accept nurturing because of a deeply held belief that the Inner Child who is going to be nurtured is wrong or bad. When we were small children, we might have decided that the needy ("baby") part of us is evil or bad. Children sometimes decide this when they hear about how hard it is to take care of a baby. Receiving nurturing may also activate the feelings we weren't allowed to experience in childhood. Remember, you can do this even if you're scared and it's all right not to do it. *On a very deep level, you know what's best for you.* Be sure to discuss your feelings and the reasons for them with at least three other members of your small group before you make your decision.

If you are already participating in an exercise and get so uncomfortable that you feel you must stop, do what you feel is right for you — and discuss it later.

8. *I will take turns giving and receiving.*

For many Adult Children, it's easier to give than to receive. Receiving or giving nurturing often releases strong emotions. Sometimes, when people finally get what they need, they suddenly feel the pain of missing so much in the past. Even just thinking about receiving or giving nurturing may rekindle memories that are so painful they seem unbearable.

If you experience strong emotions, allow yourself to express them and allow others in your group to support you. Emotions that are stifled tend to build up and cause problems. Emotions that are expressed and released tend to dissipate. Remembering your feelings about being abused can be very uncomfortable. You did survive that abuse, however, and, although your memories are painful, you now have many more resources to help you cope with the pain. Remembering your experience and feeling the emotions associated with it helps you to integrate what happened to you. The emotions will dissipate, and you will no longer need to arrange your life to avoid remembering painful experiences.

If you are in therapy, be sure to discuss strong emotional responses with your therapist. If you're not in therapy, this may be a good time to seek a professional who can help you work through the issues you're uncovering.

9. *I will take risks after I have examined the safety of the situation.*
When you feel afraid to do something, to give or receive nurturing, or to share feelings and experiences, answer these questions:

- What would have happened if I had done this as a child?
- Is that likely to happen in this situation?
- What have I observed happening to others who've done similar things in this situation?
- What's the worst thing that could possibly happen to me in this situation if I take the risk? What would I do if that happened to me? (Remember, you have many more resources now than you did when you were a child.)

It's important to proceed slowly and test the safety of any new situation. Healthy trust builds gradually. Don't give your trust to others until you have some evidence about what they will do with it. When you are considering a risk, share your answers to these questions with other members of your group and ask them for any additional help you need.

10. *I will follow the instructions of the Timekeeper even if I want to keep working in a particular area.*
This program will stimulate many thoughts and feelings. You may want to continue to discuss something even after you're told to stop. In order to complete the many activities in the time allotted, it's important to honor the time schedule. You can always continue your discussion of a particular topic after the session is over. When making time commitments outside of the session, please be aware of your own boundaries and those of others.

11. *I will not engage in any sexual activity with any member of the program with whom I do not already have a committed sexual relationship. I will keep this agreement for the duration of the program and for six months after the last session.*
Adult Children have great difficulty with intimacy and sometimes try to escape from the discomfort of intimacy by engaging in sexual activity, confusing the two. When we parent each other in this program, we are truly opening ourselves to moments of real closeness and may wish to express this closeness sexually. Acting on such impulses can damage your Inner Child. Having a sexual relationship with someone who is parenting you can seem incestuous and abusive to your Inner Child, even though on a social level you are two consenting adults. Emotional issues tend to get very confused when people try to combine the roles of parent and lover in a program such as this. To protect everyone involved, it is imperative to refrain from sexual activity until the program is over and you are certain that you are making decisions from the grown-up part of yourself.

12. *I will be responsible for honoring my commitments. I will attend every session unless an emergency or some other extremely good reason keeps me*

*away. If I do not attend, I will communicate this to other members of my group at the earliest possible time. In the event of an emergency, I will communicate with at least one member of my group before the group meets.*

All of the protective behaviors learned by children who grow up in dysfunctional families are reinforced by an unpredictable environment. Each time an agreement is not kept, it reminds you of your original family experience. To keep our environment safe for everybody's Inner Child, we do the best we can to avoid surprises. Your presence provides safety and consistency for others, as well as proving to your own Inner Child that you will be there for him or her whenever you're needed. If you know what to expect and the reasons for the changes, you will feel safer.

13. *I agree to accept reminders from others if I am not keeping these agreements.*

14. *I agree to remind others if I notice that they are not keeping these agreements.*

It is not shameful to forget an agreement. Reminders should be gentle, respectful and direct, since they are for the benefit and protection of everyone. (Example: "Joe, remember that we agreed not to laugh when someone talks about something that was probably very painful.") If you find you are consistently unable or unwilling to keep the agreements, it may be that this program is not appropriate for you at this time.

## Agreements For Creating Safety, Trust And Consistency

1. When I participate in this program, I agree to do my best to keep the following agreements.
2. I will be responsive to others.
3. I will tell the truth about my own experiences.
4. I will keep confidential anything I learn about others in this program.
5. I will use the healthy part of myself to nurture others during the program. If I have doubts or questions, I will get clarification before proceeding.
6. I will nurture in the ways suggested by the program and will discuss deviations from the instructions with at least three other people before deciding what to do.
7. I will accept the nurturing that is offered in the program. If at any time I do not wish to do so, I will discuss this with at least three other members of the program and then make my own decision about what I'm going to do.
8. I will take turns giving and receiving.
9. I will take risks *after* I have examined the safety of the situation.
10. I will follow the instructions of the timekeeper even if I want to keep working in a particular area.
11. I will not engage in any sexual activity with any member of the program with whom I do not already have a committed sexual relationship. I will keep this

agreement for the duration of the program and for six months after the last
session.

12. I will be responsible for honoring my commitments. I will attend every session
unless an emergency or some other extremely good reason keeps me away. If
I do not attend I will communicate this to other members of my group at the
earliest possible time. In the event of an emergency I will communicate with
at least one member of my group before the group meets.

13. I agree to accept reminders from others if I am not keeping these agreements.

14. I agree to remind others if I notice that they are not keeping these agreements.

_____

(Signature)                                                                        (Date)

## Continuing This Program

The remainder of the program consists of 12 *Parenting Each Other*
sessions.

The exercises in each session develop a theme based on the developmental
needs of a child at a particular age. Many of the exercises are designed to be
done in groups of six participants. Other exercises are designed to be done
with partners you will choose from within the whole group.

The materials you bring will include things like pillows, toys, books and
games that will be used as props to make it easier to parent each other. Bring
your workbook to each session.

In order to attend the next session (Session 3) of this program, which will
be the first of the *Parenting Each Other* sessions, a person should have:

Attended this session and the previous one, or have thoroughly studied the first
two sessions in the workbook, and have made a commitment to keep the agreements.

*After the first Parenting Each Other Parenting Session, no new members
may be added to the group.*

Materials you will need for the next session are:

Your *Parenting Each Other* workbook.
Your Self-Assessment Questionnaire.
Shoes with laces and socks. (You may wear them.)
A sweater or jacket. (You may wear it.)

## Between Sessions

Read Chapter 7, "The Treatment Environment," in *Recovery From Co-
dependency: It's Never Too Late To Reclaim Your Childhood.* Continue your
journal.

## Closing Song

We will now have our closing song, "The Greatest Love of All." You'll find the words on page 15. When the song is over, please help put the room back in order. Please form a large circle, join hands and sing along with the tape.

# *Parenting Sessions*

## SESSION 3

# CREATING BOUNDARIES

Your two-year-old Inner Child needs to learn that he or she is a separate person. We address this issue first because the way a two-year-old learns to become a separate person is by saying no and refusing to do what others want her to do. This skill is imperative for an Adult Child to learn in order to participate safely in this program: You must be able to say no to things that are bad for you. If some part of the program feels wrong or inappropriate, this skill can be used to protect your own boundaries.

### SELF-ASSESSMENT QUESTIONNAIRE

Review your responses to items 8 through 13 in the Self-Assessment Questionnaire that you filled out after the first session. (p. 12)

If any response to items 8 through 13 is seven or below, you may have difficulty with your boundaries.

### BOUNDARIES

Most Adult Children have difficulty with boundaries. All of these items reflect the outcome of the parenting you received when you were two, trying to establish that you were a separate person from your parents.

We all have boundaries, although we may be unwilling to acknowledge them clearly to other people or even ourselves. We have already made choices about what's right for us and what's not right for us. If we hadn't, we wouldn't be attending this meeting. Often, though, we make choices about boundaries and pretend we haven't made those choices. When we "forget" to do things we don't want to do, we are setting boundaries without taking responsibility for what we are doing. We may not know that we can clearly and directly refuse to do the things we don't want to do.

When we were two-year-olds, we needed to learn that the people around were not upset when we were asserting our own limits by saying "No!" or "I don't want to!" If we didn't learn this, we avoid doing things we don't want to do by forgetting or procrastinating. When we procrastinate, we often feel that there's something wrong with us. We may not even recognize that the problem is caused by a part of us which doesn't want to do or think about something. If there's an expensive garment we really don't like wearing, for example, and we keep forgetting to take it to the cleaners, then we don't have to pay any attention to the fact that we don't like it anymore. Most Adult Children don't realize that it's okay not to *want* to do something and that we can choose to do it anyway.

## Worksheet #9: Procrastination

Complete only Number (1) on Worksheet #9, then wait for further instructions from the Timekeeper.

(1) List five things you've been meaning to do but haven't got around to, things you've been procrastinating about. (If you don't have five items, choose some things you have procrastinated about in the past.)

1. _____

2. _____

3. _____

4. _____

5. _____

STOP! Follow the Timekeeper's instructions. If you have trouble following the verbal instructions, they are written in the SHARING EXERCISE section following Worksheet #9. Do not go on with the worksheet until the Timekeeper tells you to.

(2) For each item, list a reason why at least some part of you *doesn't want to do it.*

1. _____

2. _____

3. _____

4. _____

5. _____

(3) How did I feel when I said aloud that I didn't want to do each item?

1. _____

2. _____

3. _____

4. _____

5. _____

(4) How did I feel when I was told it's okay not to want to do each item on my list?

1. _____

2. _____

3. _____

4. _____

5. _____

(5) What will actually happen if I never do each item on my list?

1. _____

2. _____

3. _____

4. _____

5. _____

STOP! Follow the Timekeeper's instructions.
(6) Decide whether *or not* you are going to do each item on your list. If you choose to complete an item, decide on and list a date for its completion.

I choose to    I choose not to    (circle one)    complete #1 by _____.

I choose to    I choose not to    (circle one)    complete #2 by _____.

I choose to    I choose not to    (circle one)    complete #3 by _____ .

I choose to    I choose not to    (circle one)    complete #4 by _____ .

I choose to    I choose not to    (circle one)    complete #5 by _____ .

### SHARING EXERCISE

Follow the Timekeeper's instructions. If you need further clarification, refer to this section.

Share your list [Item 1 on your Worksheet] in your group. Now, taking turns, restate the first item on your list by preceding it with "I don't want to . . . ." Say this aloud to the rest of your group.

For example: "I don't want to clean my closets." As soon as you've finished saying this, the person on your right says to you, "It's okay not to want to . . . (do the thing you've been avoiding, e.g., clean your closets)." Please notice that this is *not* saying you don't have to clean your closets. It is saying that your feelings of not wanting to clean your closets are valid and accepted. You don't have to have any particular kind of feeling.

Continuing around the circle, the person on your right then says, for example, "I don't want to pick up my mother at the airport." The person on his or her right then says, "You don't have to want to pick up your mother at the airport." Continue around the group until everyone has completed all of the items on their list.

Take five minutes to quickly jot down the answers to questions (2), (3), (4) and (5) on Worksheet #9. Briefly share the answers to these questions.

Now, complete number (6) on your Worksheet. For each item, decide whether or not you are ever going to do it. If the consequence of not doing something is one you're willing to accept, it's perfectly all right to say, "I'm not going to do this."

Now go around the group again, and for each item on your list, say either, "I am going to . . . (clean my closets, pay my taxes, etc.)" or "I am not going to . . . (clean my closets, pay my taxes, etc.)" As you complete these tasks during the course of the program, please report these completions to other people in the program, especially members of the small group with whom you shared your commitment.

## Centering Ritual

Ultimately, we need to learn to love and accept all the parts of ourselves. To remind ourselves why, let's sing together the song "The Greatest Love of All." Form a circle, join hands, and listen carefully to the words of the song as you sing.

When the song is over, return to your seats in your small group area and prepare to experience what it's like to have the normal behaviors of a two-year-old child responded to with love, support and appropriate limits.

## Visualization

*Sit in a comfortable position. Take several deep breaths. Let them out slowly. Now inhale and exhale, and on each inhalation say to yourself "I am . . ." On the exhale, say to yourself, "relaxed." "I am . . . relaxed . . . I am . . . relaxed." Keep repeating this silently.*

Imagine now that you are two-year-old Terri. You live with your mommy and daddy and your big brother, Jimmy. Your big brother is five. You're at the grocery store sitting in the shopping cart. Daddy is pushing the cart while Mommy is putting lots of things into it. You say, "I want that," and Daddy puts a box of crackers in your hands. You look at it, shake it and chew on a corner of the box. You see the cookies, say "Cookie" and throw the box down. Daddy grabs the box and puts it into the shopping cart, and Mommy hands you a cookie from the lady in the bakery. You munch happily, getting cookie crumbs all over your clothes and watching all of the interesting sights.

You see somebody with an ice cream cone and say, "Ice cream," and start to drop the cookie. Jimmy takes the cookie and says, "I'll eat it," and Daddy gives you back the cookie, saying, "Yes, that's ice cream. This is your cookie." You whimper, and Dad takes the cookie and Mom hands you a small rubber toy from her purse. You say, "No! Cookie!" Dad returns the cookie to you and takes the toy away. Finally you're in the checkout lane, just sitting there. The cookie is gone, and you struggle to climb out of the cart. "Down," you say. Mommy lifts you out and says, "Stay close." You hold her hand and look around. You start to take things off the shelf. Daddy says, "That's not for you," and picks you up and bounces you. You giggle with delight. Daddy puts you down, Mommy takes your hand, and as Daddy pushes the grocery cart to the car, you hold Mommy's hand while walking out of the store. You see a big, shaggy dog tied to a post outside and stop to say hello. Mommy holds your hand and lets you gently pet the dog. She then says, "It's time to go," and you say, "No." She says, "Say goodbye to the doggie." You wave and she picks you up and carries you to the car and puts you in the car seat, straps you in, and off you go with Jimmy strapped in next to you.

Back home, Mommy and Daddy take things out of grocery bags, making big piles. You take a bag and some cans and put them in and out of the bag. Suddenly things don't work. You start to cry. Mommy picks you up and puts you in the high chair and gives you a glass of milk. You say, "No." Mommy says, "Okay" and takes the milk away. You say "Milk." She asks, "You want it?" You say, "No. Milk." Mommy gives it to you, and you drink it. Then she picks you up and says, "Nap time." You say, "No." Mommy changes your diaper and puts you in your crib, with the side down, and says, "It's time for a nap." Whimpering, you say again, "No." Mom my hands you some books and a toy telephone, says, "Just stay here quietly," and walks out of the room. You grab your favorite blanket, and put your thumb in your mouth. You start to play with the telephone, and before you know it, you're asleep.

Imagining you're Terri, notice how you feel when you want something . . . how you feel about wanting something different from what Mommy and Daddy want you to have. Notice how you feel about yourself. Notice how you feel about Mommy . . . about Daddy. Do you feel safe? Comfortable?

Now gradually bring your awareness back to the room. Open your eyes when you're ready and spend a few minutes writing about your experience. Don't worry about spelling or grammar or punctuation — just write. Now share your experience with other members of your group.

If you drifted off during some part of the visualization and missed the content of it, please go back and read the visualization before entering the discussion.

## Group Discussion

Discuss the answers to these questions with your small group. As Terri:

- How do you feel about wanting what you want when you want it?
- How do you feel about wanting something different from what Mommy and Daddy want you to have?
- How do you feel about you?
- How do you feel about Mommy?
- How do you feel about Daddy?
- Do you feel safe? Why or why not?
- Do you feel comfortable? Why or why not?
- What is Terri learning about boundaries?
- What is the message that Terri is being given by both her parents about wanting what she wants?
- What are her parents communicating about her right to say no?
- How do you think she'll feel about saying no when she's a grownup?
- What happened to you when you said no when you were small? If you don't know, guess.
- How does this affect you now?

## Nurturing Exchange

In this exercise, you will give and receive parenting. You will give with one partner and you will receive from another partner. This avoids the confusion so many of us experienced of having to be the parent to our parents. *During this program you should avoid exchanging parenting with anyone with whom you have a committed intimate relationship.* If you are sharing the group with a "significant other," you can simply make sure to be in a different pairing or small group for your parenting and Nurturing Exchanges.

## INSTRUCTIONS FOR THE PARENTER

As a parenter, your task is to get your two-year-old ready to go with you to the grocery store. You will need to help your two-year-old put on shoes and socks and a coat. As a parenter, remember that you have two jobs: one is to provide a loving, supportive and safe environment for your two-year-old; the other is to get to the grocery store and get the items you need to prepare a meal. Remember that your two-year-old is very small, is naturally self-centered, loves you and is dependent on you. She is also trying to be different from you and needs to avoid cooperating with you in order to feel her differentness. You may tell her anything that is true and that she can understand. You may not lie to her. You may touch her gently or playfully. You may not use force. In real life you would be able to pick up your two-year-old and place her where you wanted her to be. You may distract your two-year-old with toys or games to help accomplish your task.

*Don't ever* say anything that indicates there is anything wrong with the child or that is shaming or blaming. If she says "I don't want to," tell her "It's okay not to want to," and attempt to put her shoe, sock or jacket on anyhow. If she runs away, chase her playfully, saying "I'm gonna get you!" or wait for her to come back. Ask which sock or shoe she wants to put on first. Ask if she wants to put each item on herself or if she wants you to put it on for her. Go ahead and dress her while talking about something else. "Do you want to ride the rocking horse at the store?" or "We're going to see Grandma." Offer to play "This Little Piggy" before you put on each sock. Do whatever works.

Be sure your physical environment is safe. Move breakable or sharp objects out of the way. Remember, your task here is to do the very best you can and to help your partner have the experience of being nurtured with appropriate limits. You are both here to learn and grow, not to be the first ones to the store.

## INSTRUCTIONS FOR THE TWO-YEAR-OLD

As a two-year-old, it's your task to be you. Remember Terri. What Terri wanted changed quickly from one moment to the next. As a two-year-old, you depend on your parenter, and his or her approval and love is very important to you. You are curious about your world and want to explore almost everything. You love to say no and play the game of doing the opposite of what you're told.

You also love to please. You need affection. You are too little to understand trying to trick or get back at or hurt your parenter in any way. You know how to have temper tantrums or get very stiff or very flexible to resist control.

You don't care about taking care of your parent. It's his or her job to take care of you and you know it. You do like going to the grocery store; you just don't like being dressed. In this exercise, your objective is to experience what it's like to receive appropriate parenting when you are two years old. There are no prizes for getting to the grocery store last. You will return to your adult state of consciousness when told "It's time to grow up now." Before you begin, remove your shoes and socks and give them to your parenter.

**IMPORTANT!** If you have any reservations or hesitation about participating in this exercise, either as a parenter or as a two-year-old, this is the time to discuss your concerns with others in your group. Most people feel a little silly doing this kind of exercise. Feeling silly is not a good reason to avoid participation. If after consultation you choose not to participate, please observe what happens with another small group. If the numbers are uneven, you may assist someone else in parenting a two-year-old. However, no parenter should be responsible for more than one two-year-old.

If you are participating in a Nurturing Exchange (as with any exercise) and get so uncomfortable that you feel you must stop, do so, and discuss the problem with your partner.

## Doing It

Choose a partner, decide roles and proceed with the exchange, following the Timekeeper's instructions.

You will have 10 minutes for the first parenting experience, the first half of the Nurturing Exchange. At the end of this period, each of you take a piece of paper and spend a few minutes writing about your experience. When you've completed your writing, share your experience with your partner.

After you've shared, parenters go to one side of the room and former two-year-olds to the other side. Now choose a new partner from the other group. If you were the child first, you will now be a parenter and vice versa. Read the instructions that belong to your new role. When the Timekeeper says to start, be sure that the physical environment is safe again.

Take 10 minutes for the exercise, write again and share again. When everyone has completed the exchange, return to your small group. Choose two people and exchange phone numbers. If you wish to talk about anything that comes up during the week, call each other and share.

## Between Sessions

Experiment with some of these optional activities.

Read Chapter 13, "Separation Stage," in *Recovery From Co-dependency: It's Never Too Late To Reclaim Your Childhood.*

Read aloud, or have someone read to you, one or all of the following books:

*The Story Of Ferdinand,* Munro Leaf.
*The Tough Princess,* Martin Waddell and Patrick Bensen.
*Pippi Longstocking,* Astrid Lindgren.
*Mrs. Piggle Wiggle,* Betty MacDonald.
*Green Eggs And Ham,* Dr. Seuss.

Practice saying "No!" or "I don't want to!" in private, aloud, at least 20 times a day. You can do this when you're in your car, when you're in the bathroom or when you're home alone. You can say things like, "No, I don't want to drive in this traffic. No, I don't want to do the dishes. No, I don't want to go to this meeting," or whatever else it is you don't want to do.

Keep a journal of any thoughts you have relating to the experiences you've had in this program.

Be aware of anything you choose to do that you don't want to do. You might want to make a note of it in your journal.

If you are procrastinating about anything, each day go to that project and look at it, pick it up, touch it and say, "I don't want to do this." Then if you can, say to yourself, "It's okay not to want to do this."

Parent your own Inner Child the way you parented your partner in the Nurturing Exchange.

## Preparation For The Next Session

Bring some toys suitable for a one-year-old child. These can be things that make noise, things that stack or things with interesting textures. They don't need to be "real" toys that are bought in a toy store. Scraps of interesting fabric are fine, as are pots, pans, spoons — anything that would be interesting to touch or taste and large enough not to be swallowed or choke a grown-up-sized baby. Stuffed animals and favorite blankets are excellent. Baby pacifiers are great, too. Papers that can be crumpled and tissues that can be taken out of boxes and torn into little pieces are also great exploratory toys. Use your imagination.

Don't bring more toys than will fill a large grocery bag.

## Closing Song

We will end the meeting with a new song, "I Love Myself" by Jai Josefs. Form a circle with all of the participants in the program, join hands and sing along with the tape.

## I LOVE MYSELF
### by Jai Josefs

I love myself the way I am;
There's nothin' I need to change.
I'll always be the perfect me; there's nothing to rearrange.
I'm beautiful, I'm capable of bein' the best me I can,
And I love myself — just the way I am.

I love you just the way you are;
There's nothin' you need to do.
When I feel the love inside myself, it's easy to love you.
Behind your fears, your rage of tears,
I see your shining star;
And I love you just the way you are.

I love the world the way it is;
'Cuz I can clearly see
That all the things I judge are done by people just like me.
So, 'til the birth of peace on Earth
That only Love can bring,
I'll help it grow by loving everything.

I love myself the way I am;
And still I want to grow;
The change outside can only come when deep inside I know
I'm beautiful, I'm capable of bein' the best me I can,
And I love myself — just the way I am.
I love myself just the way I am.

---

# SESSION 4

---

# I Don't Know
# What I Want

---

Toddlers need to explore their sensory environment in order to learn which things appeal to them and which don't. This creates a foundation for knowing what they want throughout life. Adult Children seldom know what they want. For Adult Children, this important basic training either never existed or was lost. Instead, we have learned to figure out what others want and respond to that. Safely exploring your current sensory environment helps you to relearn what you want.

## SELF-ASSESSMENT QUESTIONNAIRE

Review your responses to questions 4 through 7 (p. 12). If you circled seven or below, you probably learned to do something other than explore your environment when you were between nine and 18 months old.

### Worksheet #10:  Making Choices

Most of us who didn't learn by exploring as toddlers have great difficulty knowing what we want and don't want today. Answering these questions will help you recognize how you make choices in your daily life.

(1) How do you decide what to eat? (Mark all the answers that fit.)

_____ I look in the kitchen, see what's available and eat that.
_____ I think about what I like ahead of time, keep it available and eat it when I feel like it.
_____ Someone chooses for me, gives it to me and I eat whatever's in front of me.
_____ I plan meals well in advance and eat what's planned.
_____ I think about what I want, choose a restaurant that has it and I go there to eat.
_____ I go along wherever others decide to go and eat what they eat.
_____ Other _____.

I think the reason I act this way is _____

_____

How do you usually feel about your choice? (Circle all that apply.)

mad      sad      glad      scared      interested      excited      bored

impatient      guilty      ashamed      indifferent      safe      comfortable

Other _____

(2) When you go to a new place such as a museum, amusement park, shopping mall, street fair or market, how do you decide what to do? (Mark any answers that fit.)

_____ I explore systematically.
_____ I go to see just one thing and then leave.
_____ I look at a map first and then decide what to do.
_____ I wander from place to place at random.
_____ I carefully examine the details of each store or exhibit before I go on to the next.
_____ I walk through the whole place quickly and then decide what to do.

Other _____
_____ I behave differently when I am alone than when I am with other people.

The difference is _____

I think the reason I act this way is _____

_____

How do you usually feel about your choice? (Circle all that apply.)

mad      sad      glad      scared      interested      excited      bored

impatient      guilty      ashamed      indifferent      safe      comfortable

Other _____

(3) When I first arrive at an unfamiliar place to spend a night away from home:

The first thing I want to do is _____

The second thing I want to do is _____

I try to avoid _____

I think the reason I act this way is _____

When I do these things, I feel _____

I behave differently when I am alone than when I am with other people.

The difference is _____

(4) When I arrive at a natural place — in the woods, the seashore, the mountains, etc.

The first thing I want to do is _____

The second thing I want to do is _____

I try to avoid _____

I think the reason I act this way is _____

When I do these things, I feel _____

I behave differently when I am alone than when I am with other people.

The difference is _____

### SHARING EXERCISE

When you've finished answering these questions, share your answers in your small group. Have each person share the answer to the first question, then the second, etc. That way everyone will have the opportunity to share even if you don't get through all the questions. As people share, be sure to acknowledge them by giving them your full attention and thanking them for their input.

## Centering Ritual

Ultimately, we need to learn to love and accept all the parts of ourselves. To remind ourselves why, let's sing together "The Greatest Love of All" (p. 15). Form a circle, join hands, and listen carefully to the words of the song as you sing.

Now return to your seat and prepare to experience what it's like to have the normal behaviors of a one-year-old child responded to with love, support and appropriate limits.

## Visualization

*Sit in a comfortable position. Take several deep breaths. Let them out slowly. Now inhale and exhale, and on each inhalation say to yourself "I am . . ." On the exhale, say to yourself, "relaxed." "I am . . . relaxed . . . I am . . . relaxed." Keep repeating this silently.*

Imagine you're Lauren. You're one year old. You're a great crawler. You can pull yourself up and hold on to the edges of furniture and look up over the seat and see what's there. You can pull yourself up on low tables, too. You're just beginning to walk, but crawling's a lot faster. You are very, very interested in your world. You're home with Mom, feeling safe and secure as you sit on the kitchen floor in front of an open cabinet and pull out interesting objects of different shapes that fit inside each other and make wonderful noises when they bang together and when they hit the floor. Mom hands you a spoon and takes your hand in hers and bangs the spoon on one of the pots. You giggle and coo. Mom smiles and says, "That's a pretty noise," and goes back to what she's doing.

You get bored with banging, put the spoon in your mouth and suck on it for a while. It feels good on your sore gums. Then you drop it and crawl over to some other cabinets and try to get them open. They don't open. You lose interest quickly and spot the cat curled up in one corner. With a cry of glee you crawl over to her and start to pull at her skin and fur. She purrs, and you feel how wonderfully soft the fur feels. Isn't that interesting?

The telephone rings. Mom is going into the next room and you can't see her anymore. You stay with the cat for a moment and listen to Mom's voice. Anxiously you look around: Where is she? You start to crawl through the doorway. You spot her and she sees you and smiles. You crawl over and try to climb her leg. Her slacks feel soft. She picks you up and holds you while she talks on the phone. You cuddle into her arms for a minute. Then you see her earring, bright and shiny. You reach for it, and she takes your hand and helps you pat her earring. You then try for her glasses and she catches your hand and says, "No, those are not for you." She crumples a piece of paper from the pad in front of her and hands it to you. You feel it, taste it and drop it on the floor.

Mom finishes her conversation and carries you over to a corner filled with toys. She goes and sits down with some papers (you don't know that it's the term paper she's writing). You pick up a fuzzy ball and roll it across the floor. That's interesting. You crawl after it, pick it up, rub your face on it and giggle. Then you notice something on the floor. It's small and a different color than the rest of the carpet. You carefully pick it up and put it in your mouth. Mom comes over and says, "No, that's not for eating," and holds her hand for you to spit it out. She hands you something that moves and makes interesting noises. You watch it for a while and then crawl over to the couch where Mom is sitting with her papers. You pull yourself up and reach for the papers. She moves them to where you can't reach and tickles you. Again you giggle gleefully.

Mom gets up and goes back into the kitchen. You discover the smooth surface of the coffee table with a large, heavy object on it. You reach for it and try to push, but it doesn't move, so you lose interest. You begin to whimper. Mom calls, "I'm in here." You follow the sound of her voice and discover those interesting shiny objects and the spoon you'd forgotten. You sit down and bang contentedly for a while. Then something happens. You feel bad. You start to cry. Mom picks you up and says, "Are you hungry?" and sits down in the rocking chair with you, and lets you nurse. You snuggle contentedly into her arms.

Imagining you're Lauren, notice how you feel when you see something interesting within your reach . . . Notice how you feel when you can't seem to have something you want . . . How long does the feeling last? Notice how you feel when you're alone. Notice how you feel when you can see Mom but not touch her. Notice how you know when you want something. Notice how you know when you're through with it and don't want it anymore.

Gradually bring your awareness back to the room. Open your eyes when you're ready and write about your experience. If you drifted off during the visualization, read it in your workbook before beginning the discussion.

## Group Discussion

Have one person read the question and each group member answer *briefly,* then go on to the next question. Follow the Timekeeper's instructions. If you don't have time to discuss all the questions, think about them after the session.

- What does Lauren learn about her ability to control her own surroundings? (Lauren is too immature to clearly differentiate herself from her mother or her environment.)
- Does Lauren seem to know what she wants?
- How could a child Lauren's age learn to not know what she wants?
- How could Lauren learn that it's more important to please her mother than to know what she wants?
- How could Lauren learn that it is not safe to explore her world?
- What do you think are the most important things to do when taking care of a one-year-old?
- How do you think you were parented when you were Lauren's age? (How many children were in your family? How old were they when you were a year old?

Who was your caretaker? What happened to you?) You may know some of these things by remembering how your caretakers treated younger siblings, or you may be able to figure it out by how they treat their grandchildren.

• How does what you learned then influence your life now?
• What do you wish had happened that didn't happen?
• What kind of experience does your Inner Child still need to have in order to feel as safe and secure and interested in the world as Lauren is?

## Nurturing Exchange

During this Nurturing Exchange exercise, it is very important that the physical environment receive careful attention. Each person will have the opportunity to explore the world as Lauren did. You will have the opportunity to experience yourself as a one-year-old, focusing exclusively on what is appealing to you and your own feelings. The parenter will be completely responsible for your safety as an explorer.

### INSTRUCTIONS FOR THE PARENTER

It's your job to create a situation where it is safe for your explorers to examine the world on their own initiative. Examine the objects that were brought to make sure they're safe for an exploring child, then scatter them in various locations where a crawling child will encounter them.

It's not your job to entertain your explorer. Repeatedly handing things to a young child can undercut the child's initiative. Let the child go after what he or she wants.

It's all right to play games of giving and taking and giving back if they are played at the initiative of your charge. If your explorer sits still, it is *not* your responsibility to give him or her things of interest. Simply wait until the child decides what to do next. Your job is to be responsive, not to initiate.

When the child is about to do something dangerous or destructive, distract him or her with anything that seems interesting. You might try rattling keys or crumpling paper or presenting a new toy to divert your explorer's attention. You may also have to physically intervene by placing your body between the child and the dangerous object or situation. Do your best to limit the use of the word no. Save it for a particularly dangerous situation when you can't get there fast enough or when you cannot otherwise resolve the situation.

When explorers come to you, stroke their backs, faces, shoulders, anything that's presented. Remember that your charge is a precious child who needs your love and attention to grow up to be healthy. Talk to your explorers, although they are not really old enough to understand most of what you say. Your tone of voice and facial expression are more important than your words.

Before you start, look around the physical environment and remove anything that could easily be broken by a large-sized baby. It's important to babyproof the house rather than houseproof the baby, so babyproof your environment as much as you possibly can. Put dangerous things in high places, in closets or behind barriers. If your baby puts something in his or her mouth which appears dangerous, do something gentle to remove it. Don't be too concerned about dirt. Distraction is a good plan.

### INSTRUCTIONS FOR THE EXPLORER

Remember how small you are. You're only a year old. You have very little language, although you probably understand the word no. You are attracted by energy: colorful things, moving things, unfamiliar things. Your hands, your mouth and your eyes are your main tools for finding out about the world. You can crawl well. You walk unsteadily.

When you're being little, focus on what interests you. If nothing interests you, take your time, look around you and notice what attracts your attention before you move toward it. If something gets in your way that might be of equal interest, pay attention to that. When something you're exploring no longer interests you, look around for the next thing that holds the most attraction for you.

Making sounds is natural, although you may know only one or two words. Do your best not to think about what's going on in the room and not think about what's safe and what isn't safe — just go for what interests you. Allow yourself to be sidetracked if the distraction is interesting to you. If you feel upset, whimper or cry.

People are interesting to explore, as are the various toys in the room. You have no concept of what belongs to you or what belongs to somebody else, so anything is fair game. Stay with something as long as it feels right. Remember, strokes from your parenter are very important. You feel safe exploring as long as your parenter is within range. You may find yourself waiting for someone to give you something to do. If that's the case, simply stay still or express your discomfort with noise or tears.

Remember, this is not an exercise to try to thwart your caretaker. It's simply about finding out what is right for you. You are too small to remember much about the existence of an object when you can't see it or feel it. You're too immature to persist in looking for something once it disappears.

**IMPORTANT!** If you have any reservations about participating in this exercise, discuss them in your small group. If you choose not to participate, observe participants closely and notice your own feelings in response.

If you are participating in a Nurturing Exchange and get so uncomfortable that you feel you must stop, do so, and discuss the problem with your partner.

## Doing It

Follow the instructions of the Timekeeper and do the activities.

You will have ten minutes for each half of this exercise. The Timekeeper will tell you when to start and when to stop. At the end of the exercise, the parenter will tell the explorer, "It's time to grow up now." When the explorer has grown up, each of you spend a few minutes writing about your experience and then share with each other what it was like to do this activity. After a brief break, choose a new partner who had the role opposite to you in the first part of the exercise. Switch roles and read the instructions for your new role. Repeat the exercise, the writing and the sharing.

## Between Sessions

Experiment with some of these optional activities:

Read: Chapter 11, "Exploratory Stage," in *Recovery From Co-dependency: It's Never Too Late To Reclaim Your Childhood.*

Have someone read aloud to you any of the following exploratory baby books:

*Pat The Bunny,* Dorothy Kunhardt.
*Madeline And The Bad Hat,* Ludwig Bemelmans.
*When You Were A Baby,* Katharine Ross.
*Nice Or Nasty: A Book Of Opposites,* Nick Butterworth.
*Very Hungry Caterpillar,* Eric Carle.
*Baby's First Book,* A Platt Munk Teddy Board Book.
*The Mouse And The Motorcycle,* Beverly Cleary.
*Babies' Book Of Babies,* Sabrina Withall.

Spend some time at a department store. Leave your money at home. Go from place to place as it interests you. Look at and touch the merchandise. If a salesperson approaches you, say, "Thank you, I'm just looking," and move on.

Explore a small area out-of-doors. Notice how many different living things there are in a square foot of grass. Look at a flower intently and carefully. Taste snow. Watch an insect walk across the ground.

Go to an unfamiliar restaurant from a different culture. Order several new foods. Taste them. If you like them, eat them. If you don't, leave them.

When you're home alone, peel a banana, put it in your hand, squeeze it, then do whatever you want with it, which may or may not include eating it.

Drive to work by an unfamiliar route.

In each of these exercises, you need to keep your own grown-up self available to protect your child as you explore. Try some exercises you come up with on your own and report back to the group about them. Remember, the objective is to notice your sensory environment and your response to it.

Write in your journal.

## Preparation For The Next Session

For the next session, bring toys and books that are suitable for a three- to four-year-old child, a preschooler. This can include crayons, coloring books and paper, trucks, dolls, hats, masks, fake noses, balloons, bubbles and costumes for imaginative play. If you have books that were favorites when you were a child, be sure to bring them. Don't bring too many different things. Fill a grocery bag and stop there.

## Closing Song

We will end the meeting with the song, "I Love Myself" by Jai Josefs (p. 40).

# SESSION 5

# LEARNING TO ASK

Asking for what you want is a fundamental skill we are all born with. We come into the world knowing how to cry when we need something. This is how we tell our caretakers that we feel uncomfortable; we're asking for help. Babies who live in healthy families don't hesitate to demand what they want. As we grow in healthy families, we learn to change these demands into requests.

Children learn that these requests sometimes get them what they want and other times they don't. Learning to accept no for an answer (sometimes) is an important part of learning to ask. Healthy adults ask for what they want. If their requests are denied, they solve the problem in a variety of other ways. Most Adult Children have learned to wait, wish for things or manipulate others, rather than asking directly.

We fear being rejected. We take rejection personally, as further evidence of our own inferiority. We have a difficult time understanding that somebody turning us down is a message about that person and his or her needs, rather than about us. In this session, we'll experience learning how to ask for what we want and how to respond when someone else says no to our requests.

## SELF-ASSESSMENT QUESTIONNAIRE

Review your responses to items 2, 6, 9, 14, 17, 18 and 25 (pp. 12-13). They are related to your level of comfort in asking for what you want.

If your responses to these questions show a pattern of seven or below, asking may be a particular problem for you. If you didn't learn how to ask appropriately when you were a child, you probably still have difficulty asking for what you want now.

In the first exercise, we'll rehearse asking for what we want as grownups.

## Worksheet #11: Not Asking

Using a separate sheet of paper please make a list of several things that you have wanted but haven't asked for recently. Recently could be today, this week, this month, even this year.

Things Adult Children typically don't ask for are: praise for doing a job well, information for solving a problem, appreciation for extra effort, having things fixed when they go wrong — for example, asking to have your food heated up in a restaurant when it's served cold. Respond to the following statements for each item on your list:

I wanted to ask for _____

I could have asked (name of person) _____

I didn't ask because _____

Instead of asking, I _____

Decide which item on your Worksheet you want to explore further in this exercise.

### EXERCISE: LEARNING TO ASK, PART 1

#### INSTRUCTIONS FOR THE SENDER

Pretend your partner is the person you didn't ask for what you wanted and this time make the request aloud. Take the item on your list you want to explore further and tell the receiver, very briefly, the person you are having them represent. Then ask aloud for what you want.

#### INSTRUCTIONS FOR THE RECEIVER

Your job is to be an active listener. Demonstrate that you heard the sender's request by mirroring back the sender's words. (Active listening is an extremely valuable technique for making certain that you know your communication has been received. It is discussed in detail in Dr. Thomas Gordon's *Parent Effectiveness Training.*) When a request is made, simply say back to the person your understanding of their request.

For example, if someone asks, "Will you give me a ride downtown at 3:00?" you respond, "You want me to give you a ride downtown at 3:00, is that correct?" The sender can say either yes, or if that is not correct, correct it. If necessary, the receiver should actively listen again until the sender is clear that you understood the request.

Choose a member of your small group as a partner. Decide who will be the sender and who will be the receiver.

### EXERCISE: LEARNING TO ASK, PART 2

#### INSTRUCTIONS FOR THE SENDER

Ask again but this time be very direct about it. If the first time you asked, you said, "I would like you to do something for me," change your words to, "*Will you* do a specific thing for me?" If you asked "Will you?" the first time, this time try saying, "Will you do this specific thing at (or by) this specific time?" Change "I'd like a ride downtown" to "Will you take me downtown?" Change "Will you take me downtown?" to "Will you take me downtown at 3:00?"

#### INSTRUCTIONS FOR THE RECEIVER

Reflect back what the sender has said.

#### ADDITIONAL INSTRUCTIONS

Now each sender share with your partner what you felt each time you made the request. Receivers, share what you felt like doing in response to each request.

Now change roles and repeat the exercise.

## Group Discussion

Discuss the following questions in your small group:

- What happens when you make an indirect request? (An indirect request usually starts with your feelings or a statement about what you want, but doesn't demand action on the part of the receiver.)
- What changes when someone makes a direct request of a receiver by asking "Will you?" or by putting in a time clause?

- What were the rules about asking for what you wanted in your family-of-origin?
- How do those rules affect you in your life today?

In healthy families children learn to ask directly for what they want and to deal with the disappointment of having the requests refused. When we have trouble asking directly for what we want, we may also have difficulty turning others down when they ask for something.

## Centering Ritual

Ultimately, we need to learn to love and accept all the parts of ourselves. To remind ourselves why, let's sing together "The Greatest Love of All" (p. 15). Form a circle, join hands, and listen carefully to the words of the song as you sing.

Return to your seats. Prepare to experience what it's like to have the normal behaviors of a three-and-a-half-year-old child responding to love, support and appropriate limits.

## Visualization

Our visualization today will focus on Jamie, who is three-and-a-half and very busy learning how to ask for what she wants instead of just demanding it. He's also learning how to count other people and how to accept that sometimes he can't have what he wants and that it's all right. You may visualize Jamie as either a little boy or a little girl.

*Sit in a comfortable position. Take several deep breaths. Let them out slowly. Now inhale and exhale, and on each inhalation say to yourself "I am . . ." On the exhale, say to yourself, "relaxed." "I am . . . relaxed . . . I am . . . relaxed." Keep repeating this silently.*

Now imagine that you're Jamie. You're three-and-a-half years old and you're big. You go to preschool. Preschool is an exciting place. Three mornings every week you go to your school with four teachers and 20 to 25 other children. Today, as soon as you come in, you remember the truck you were playing with the last time you were here. You hurriedly wave goodbye to Mom, hang your coat on the hook and go to the shelf where the truck is. It's not there! You find the teacher in the toy area and say, "Mary Lou, where's the truck? I want it." Mary Lou says, "Oh, I think somebody left it in the sandbox yesterday, go look there." You do. You find the truck and decide the sandbox is a great place to play with it. You make a road and run it up and down the road.

Then it's time to sing. You want to sit next to Brian, the music teacher, but somebody's already there. You push in. Brian sees you and says, "Wait a minute, Jimmy was here first. If you want to sit here, ask Jimmy if he'll move." You ask and Jimmy says "No." You start to cry and Brian says, "Ask

Jimmy if he'll trade with you after we sing two songs." You ask, and Jimmy says "Okay." You take a different spot and sing. You remind Jimmy when it's time to trade. After singing, it's time to fingerpaint. Everybody gets a piece of paper and you say, "I want blue." Mary Lou gives you the blue finger-paints. You love squishing the paint around on the paper and seeing all the different patterns you can make. Finally you make hand prints all over.

Suddenly you think about Mom at home with your new baby brother. You feel uncomfortable and lonesome. You tell Mary Lou you want to go home. Mary Lou asks why, and you just tell her you want to go home. She says, "How 'bout a hug?" and you happily climb onto her lap and sit there while she hugs you for a few minutes. She asks if you'd like to help her get the snacks ready. You feel important and agree, and carefully put two crackers on every plate. After a snack and a rest, it's time to play outside on the playground. Shannon gets to the swing before you do and you want it. The new teacher, Jeannette, comes by and sees you looking sadly at the swingset. She reminds you that "The asking words are 'Will you.'" Jeannette tells you to ask Shannon, "Will you let me have a turn?" You ask. Shannon says, "Yes, soon." And you stand and wait impatiently until she's through swinging, and you climb on and have a great time. Brian comes by, and you ask, "Will you push me?" He says, "Just for a minute," and gives you a push and then says, "Now I have to go back inside and get things ready for later."

When Mom comes to pick you up, you run to her for a hug, and as soon as you get in the car you say, "Can we get french fries from McDonalds?" Mom says, "No, we're having peanut butter sandwiches at home." You say, "But I want french fries." Mom says, "We only get french fries one day a week, and we had them the day before yesterday." You say, "Can we go shopping and get the new Cookie Crunch cereal?" Mom says, "No, it has too much sugar in it." You sigh, think about it for a minute and say, "Will you read me *Winnie the Pooh?*" Mom says, "Okay, I'll do that as soon as we get home." You look at your little brother asleep in the car seat and look up at Mom. She reaches over and strokes your hair.

Imagining you're Jamie, notice how you feel about school . . . how you feel about your brother . . . how you feel about your mother. Notice how you feel about learning to share.

Bring your awareness back to the room.

Write about your experience. If you missed any part of the visualization, read it in your workbook.

## Group Discussion

Talk about your experience with other members of your group.
Quickly share how you felt as Jamie:

- Sitting in the car and having your hair stroked
- About your little brother

  • About school
  • About getting what you want when you want it.

Now answer these questions:

  • What did Jamie really want from his mother?
  • Was he effective about getting it?
  • What did he learn about asking for what he wants?
  • When you were a child, do you think you asked for what you wanted?
  • What would have happened if you had asked?
  • What kind of response would you have liked when you did ask for what you wanted?
  • Do you ask for what you want now?
  • What works the best to get what you want?

## Nurturing Exchange

In this exercise, your Inner Child will be three-and-a-half years old and learning the same things that Jamie is learning. You will each play, just like Jamie did, and you will each have the opportunity to parent each other in a way that enhances the self-esteem of your partner's Inner Child.

### INSTRUCTIONS FOR THE PARENTER

Your role as a parenter is to be a friendly, interested grown-up. You are not the child's original parent.

Your job is to help the preschooler learn about the world and feel good about herself or himself. Always respond in some way to each request and initiative. You are under no obligation to say yes to every request. You can say no, followed by a brief explanation. You can even say, "Wait a few minutes, I'm doing something else right now."

Your job is to enhance self-esteem. To do this, refrain from saying anything that might shame a child. Never label a preschooler or their work as good or bad. Talk about it in terms of what it is. If a child shows you a picture, comment on the colors, shapes and content. You can even talk about your own feelings: "I like that," or "That's got so much black in it, I don't like it much." If a child says to you, "Am I good or am I bad?" or "He's good," or "He's bad," say that people aren't good or bad, but sometimes they do things that other people like, or sometimes they do things people don't like.

Do not tell a preschooler that he or she is selfish for not wanting to share. If a preschooler has a favorite toy that somebody else wants, the preschooler is not obligated to share it. You can ask the preschooler to decide how long they want to play with it and when they're through to give it to the person who wants it next.

It's useful to help your preschooler learn to deal with not always getting what he wants. If you're asked to read too many books, it's okay to say, "No, I'm tired of reading. Let's do something else." Any time you refuse a request, please give a reason for refusing. Never say to a preschooler, "You want too much." Instead take responsibility for saying "I (the parenter) don't want to do that much."

You will need to set limits. If your preschooler says, "I want to play outside," you'll probably want to say no, with a reason. The reason may be that we're doing all our play inside today. Answer all requests as honestly and clearly as you can, but keep your answers short. Preschoolers don't need or like a lot of long, detailed information. You can offer to play with your preschooler or to read a story, however, let most of the initiative come from the preschooler. If the decision of the preschooler is "I don't want to do what you want to do," honor it. If you need help, say to a child, "Just a minute, I need to talk to somebody about how to tell you that," and then consult with another parenter.

## INSTRUCTIONS FOR THE PRESCHOOLER

Your role as a preschooler is to be a curious, active, social explorer. You want to learn as much as you can about the world around you, the people in it and the objects in it.

Notice what you want and ask for it. Things that you may want are: a toy somebody else is playing with; information about why someone is doing something; help doing something yourself, like getting something off a high shelf or building something; a story read to you; feedback on something that you've done.

You can ask indirectly by telling somebody something that you've observed and inviting them to have a conversation with you about it. You can also interrupt people and ask for the attention you want by starting to talk to them.

Don't be afraid to ask for things that you can't have. You need the experience of being limited and learning how it feels to be limited. Feel free to ask to go to the zoo, to play outside, to go get ice cream or anything else that occurs to you.

Do each activity as long as it interests you. When you lose interest, go on to something else.

**IMPORTANT!** Discuss any reservations you have with your group before you go on. If you choose not to participate, please stay in the room and be available to be supportive to parenters who indicate a need for help. Also observe what's going on with one or two partners, so that you'll be in a position to give additional feedback during the sharing.

58 Laurie Weiss

If you are participating in a Nurturing Exchange and get so uncomfortable that you feel you must stop, do so, and discuss the problem with your partner.

## Doing It

Choose a partner and decide who will be the child and who will be the parenter. If you choose only to observe, ask to watch one pair of partners, rather than try to watch everyone. Share your observations when the exchange ends. Just the facts, please — no critical feedback.

Place the bags of toys in various locations around the room, then follow the Timekeeper's instructions and begin to parent each other. The parenters are responsible for listening for the Timekeeper's instructions.

About three minutes before it's time to stop, the Timekeeper will tell the parenters to ask the preschoolers to put the toys in some sort of order and clear them out of the middle of the floor. The parenter tells the child to grow up on the Timekeeper's signal.

Take a few minutes to write about your experience, then share your experience with your partner. Find a new partner who played the opposite role in the first exchange and change roles. Read the instructions for your new role and repeat the Nurturing Exchange.

## Between Sessions

Experiment with some of these optional activities.

Read Chapter 4, "A Systematic Treatment Approach, Part 1: Foundations," in *Recovery From Co-dependency: It's Never Too Late To Reclaim Your Childhood.*

Go to a children's museum, if one is available, and look at the exhibits through the eyes of your preschool-age Inner Child.

Read aloud or have read to you the following books:

*David And Dog,* Shirley Hughes.
*The Velveteen Rabbit,* Margery Williams.
*Finders Keepers,* William Lipkind and Nicolas Mordvinoff.
*Make Way For Ducklings,* Robert McCloskey.
*Even If I Did Something Awful,* Barbra Shook Hazen.
*Beware The Dragons,* Sara Wilson.
*William's Doll,* Charlotte Zolotow.
*Corduroy,* Don Freeman.
*Where Did I Come From?,* Peter Mayle.

Practice asking for what you want in small, low-risk situations. Ask the grocery clerk to please give you plastic or paper bags, whatever your preference. Practice asking with the words "Will you please . . .?" instead of "I would like . . ."

Have a discussion with someone important to you and tell them you would like to practice asking for things. Tell them that they should say no if they don't want to give you what you ask for. If they agree, go ahead and practice with them.

Call a travel agent and ask them to send you information about a trip you would like to take. Ask a friend to do you a favor.

Ask someone to send you a postcard from out-of-town.

Keep a journal of what happens as you practice these optional activities.

## Preparation For The Next Session

Wear loose, comfortable clothing. Make sure the room is well supplied with pillows; you may each need to bring several. If the room is uncomfortably cool, bring a blanket as well.

## Closing Song

We will end the meeting with the song, "I Love Myself" (p. 40).

# HOLDING AND TOUCHING

We are all born pure, innocent and lovable. When our infant selves are responded to with love, wonder, appropriate holding and nurturing touch, we learn to trust the world that is made up of ourselves and our caretakers. We bond and heal the wound caused by the experience of being born and separated. As infants, the way we experience unconditional love and acceptance is through loving touch. Touch is the foundation of human experience. In dysfunctional families, babies sometimes do not receive the loving touch that is appropriate. When parents are unavailable because of addictions, unresolved grief or other trauma, babies may not learn to trust. They may not bond. They may experience an emptiness that John Bradshaw calls "the hole in the soul."

Adults can learn to recognize and appreciate the true essence or spirit of another. We can connect on an intimate level without touch. As important as this kind of connection is to us it doesn't fill the hole in the infant part of ourselves, a part which may still be longing for the nurturing touch we never received. In a single session we cannot make up for the extreme lack of nurturing some of us experienced. We can, however, create an experience in which our infant selves can begin to learn what it's like to be loved and accepted. In this session we will attempt to look beyond surface characteristics and truly appreciate and acknowledge each other. Each person will have the opportunity to be physically nurtured and held in a way that approximates the experience of an infant. Each person will be able to regulate the amount of touch he or she receives. Sexual touching *is not* permitted!

## SELF-ASSESSMENT QUESTIONNAIRE

Review your responses to items 1 through 3 (p. 12).

These questions are general indications of your experience of appropriate nurturing in the first few months of life. Low scores on these questions may indicate unmet infant needs.

As an infant, you cry when something is wrong. If you get a comforting response when you signal your distress and experience relief, then you learn to express your needs and expect the environment to respond and comfort you. Your need for touching, recognition and attention from others is a need almost as basic as the need for food and warmth. When you received that loving response as an infant, your needs were validated. As you grow, you take responsibility to make sure those needs are met throughout your life.

### SILENT APPRECIATION EXERCISE

In this exercise we will experience the power and impact of letting another human being truly acknowledge our existence. We will contact and acknowledge each other without touching or speaking.

First, form a circle including everyone in the room. Now count off by twos, (one, two, one, two, etc.) Each number one will then step inside the circle and face the number two who was on your immediate left. There should now be a double circle of people facing each other. (If numbers are uneven, put an empty chair in the outer circle to mark a space.) As the music plays, simply look into the eyes of the person you are facing. Appreciate that person. Look beyond their physical appearance and see their humanity. Look. Don't talk, don't touch, just look. Appreciate the essence of the person you are facing.

You may feel like giggling or crying or wanting to hide. You may feel elated or you may feel nothing. Whatever the feelings, do your best to continue with the exercise. Stay together until you hear the signal to move to the next person. The outer circle remains standing still, the inner circle moves to the right at the Timekeeper's signal and each person faces a new partner. (When you reach the empty space, just stand quietly until the circle moves again.) Continue this exercise until you have faced a total of at least six people in the room.

If your group is less than 12, instead of using the circle format, you may wish to simply move around freely until you have made contact with every person in the group.

When the Timekeeper signals that the exercise is complete, return to your small groups. Share your answers to the following questions:

- How did you feel during the exercise?
- Did your feelings change depending on who you were with?
- Did you reach any conclusions about yourself or other people while doing this exercise?
- Are there ways in which you can allow the time to experience the essence of people who are in your life every day?
- Has there ever been anyone in your life whom you know appreciates you for who you are as well as for what you do? If so, how do they communicate that to you?
- What can you do to let other people know that you appreciate who they are as well as what they do?
- Where do you find this kind of acknowledgment in your current life? If you don't have it currently, what can you do to create it?

## Centering Ritual

Ultimately, we need to learn to love and accept all the parts of ourselves. To remind ourselves why, let's sing together "The Greatest Love of All" (p. 15). Form a circle, join hands, and listen carefully to the words of the song as you sing.

Return to your seats and prepare to experience what it's like to have the normal behaviors of a tiny baby responded to with unconditional love and support.

## Visualization

*Sit in a comfortable position. Take several deep breaths. Let them out slowly. Now inhale and exhale, and on each inhalation say to yourself "I am . . ." On the exhale, say to yourself, "relaxed." "I am . . . relaxed . . . I am . . . relaxed." Keep repeating this silently.*

Now imagine yourself getting smaller and smaller . . . and smaller until you are no bigger than the length of your mother's arm. As you shrink, your body changes. You can no longer direct your muscles to walk. Your skin becomes exquisitely sensitive. There is no longer a memory of the past or an expectation of the future. You have become a tiny, tiny baby and the only time is right now.

You are Lyn, a tiny baby snuggled in your mother's arms. As Lyn, you feel safe and warm and protected, and all is well with your world. You're a biological creature. At this moment, all you know is that everything is fine. You wiggle a little and get even more comfortable. You don't know this, but as you wiggle, your mother looks down at you and is awed by your beauty, by your perfection, by the miracle that is you. She holds you and thinks welcoming thoughts: "I'm so glad to be able to hold you in my arms. I've waited so long for you. I'm so glad you're here. You're beautiful. I love holding you close."

She says words aloud and you hear her familiar voice. All is well in your world. You rest in a center of peace and warmth. The world is good and you don't separate yourself from the world. You are good. You belong. Your skin feels softness. You feel the familiar rhythm of your mother's heartbeat. You are peaceful and your consciousness drifts away. You know nothing of the passage of time. There's only now.

Suddenly now is no longer good. Your skin is cold, clammy. You wiggle and struggle and no one is there. There's a gnawing in your stomach. You don't know what it is. All you know is that the world is wrong and you are wrong. You stir and whimper, and then the soothing touch is back, the sounds are back. Of course, you don't understand the words: "Oh, you're wet. I'll fix it. You must be hungry. I love you, it's okay, I'll take care of you." The soothing cloud of presence envelopes you even before you're physically comfortable. Your panic turns to comfort and joy. You feel yourself being touched and you feel yourself warm again. Once more in your mother's arms, safe, you turn your face at the touch of a nipple and it's in your mouth and you're sucking. As you suck, warm milk flows into your body. The world is good. You are good.

You hear the familiar heartbeat, feel the familiar thoughts and relax into the warmth and pleasure of being welcomed and loved and cared for. You hear the familiar voice again, crooning as mother again looks at you with awe and appreciates your perfection. Other sounds come too, familiar ones that you heard even before you came into the world. Dad is close, holding Mother, although you don't know that. He, too, looks at you and admires you and can hardly wait to hold you. Other family members come and look in awe and touch gently. You feel safe and secure.

Dad picks you up and holds you. This is different. Not quite right. The smell is different. The heartbeat doesn't feel quite the same. You're too little to remember what's right, you just know. So you whimper and Dad snuggles you close. Dad's thoughts of welcome and wonder at your soft and tiny perfection flow over you. Again you relax and all is well. You love to be safe and warm and close. Each time something goes wrong and you feel the wrongness, you cry . . . and someone comes. The wrongness stays for what seems to be forever because there's only now and you cry long and hard. Always, when you cry, love and warmth surround you and the goodness comes again. After this cycle happens again and again, the goodness and rightness remain with you, and a sense of belonging and love becomes a part of your being. Let yourself relax into that sense of belonging and love and rightness and safety. (Allow a full minute here.)

And now, allow your awareness of your body to expand to your current body. Allow your awareness of your surroundings to change and allow yourself to come back to your present body and into the room. When you're ready, open your eyes.

Sit quietly for a moment or two and then write about your experience. If you missed any part of the visualization, read it in your workbook.

## Group Discussion

In a small group, take turns sharing what you've experienced. Discuss these questions:

- What kind of response does a baby need in order to feel welcome in the world?
- What kind of response does a baby need in order to feel safe?
- How do you think an infant experiences being held by someone who feels angry?
- How do you think an infant experiences being held by someone who feels afraid?
- How do you think an infant experiences being held by someone who feels sad?
- How do you think an infant experiences being left to cry for long periods of time?
- Were you welcomed and responded to as Lyn was when you were an infant?
- Were there unavoidable physical circumstances (illness, injury, handicap, etc.) that interfered with your loving treatment?
- Were there emotional circumstances in your family that interfered with your being treated as Lyn was?

## Nurturing Exchange

In this exchange you will hold and be held by another person in a safe and secure environment. The holder needs to be physically comfortable, sitting on a couch or on the floor with back support. Review the instructions carefully before you begin.

### INSTRUCTIONS FOR THE PARENTER/HOLDER

Get physically comfortable so that you can stay in one position for ten minutes. Arrange pillows to support your back and also have some sort of arrangement to support your arm that will be holding the weight of your "baby." You need to prepare yourself to hold a large body, but to see within that body the infant that was and to respond to the person you're holding as if they're small, helpless, beautiful and worthy of loving attention. You become the loving parent to this baby.

Hold the upper part of the baby's body against your chest, so that the baby's ear is against your heart and the baby can feel and hear your heartbeat. The baby's face should be turned toward you. Sometimes raising your knee can provide support for the baby. You may want a pillow under your knee if you do this. The baby is not to support his or her own weight, so you need to find a comfortable way to provide that support. Sometimes the baby will want to tuck his or her downside arm down and around you. Other times that arm will be in your lap. Before your baby gets into the psychological infant space, work together to find a comfortable physical configuration. The baby's legs usually curl toward you, the holder, as the baby is stretched out on the floor or the couch.

Make an agreement with your partner about what kind of physical touch he or she likes best. Experiment with stroking the hair, cheek and shoulder, lightly or firmly and see what feels best. A small-bodied person can easily hold a large-bodied person if you work together to adapt yourselves. When you're both comfortable, tell your partner to go ahead and relax and become little.

As you hold your baby, allow yourself to appreciate what a small, tender, helpless and wonderful infant this person once was. Stroke them gently and communicate silently and/or verbally. You want to communicate to the baby things like this: "You are welcome here; you belong. I like to be close to you and take care of you. You're wonderful just the way you are. You deserve love and attention and you can take your time and receive it. All of your feelings are okay with me. You don't have to do anything to earn this, you deserve it just because you're here."

As you hold your baby, think about the times you've seen an infant and marveled at their perfection. Think about the wonders of life and the connections we have with each other. As you hold your baby, do your best to focus your attention on his or her needs. If the baby squirms and seems uncomfortable, do your best to accommodate and create comfort and warmth again. If you can't seem to comfort the baby, stay focused on the loving thoughts and do the best you can. Holding is meant to feel good to the holder as well as the one being held. Let yourself enjoy the experience of being close.

### INSTRUCTIONS FOR THE BABY

Your goal is to allow yourself to feel nurtured by the holder or parent. You will rest in the holder's lap with your head against his or her chest, facing the holder and curling your legs toward the holder so that you can have as much physical contact as possible. Your buttocks should be next to or between the holder's legs — not on the holder's leg. Find a comfortable position where the holder can support you; try not to support yourself physically. Discuss your position and work it out with your holder before you allow your mind to drift into being "little." If there are physical problems such as a sore back, discuss them with your partner and if you need other help, get consultation. Sometimes holding needs to be modified to accommodate sore parts. Use whatever pillows and padding are necessary to make the situation comfortable.

Think about what kind of stroking you'd like from your holder before you get little. Experiment with the holder stroking your hair, your cheek, your shoulder, your back or other parts of your body. Tell the holder what feels best and then relax as much as you can. If you get uncomfortable at any time during the process, wiggle until you get comfortable again or whimper so that the holder can make adjustments. A baby doesn't communicate in words and it's up to the caretaker to figure out what's wrong and fix it. If all else fails, go ahead and use words to tell the holder what kind of adjustments need to be made.

When the holder says, "It's all right to get little now," let yourself relax as much as you can and focus on your physical experience. Focus only on your own needs. It's the holder's responsibility to take care of himself or herself. You may want to rest your head on the holder's shoulder or chest. When the holder talks, listen to the sound of the voice. It doesn't matter whether or not the words make sense. Just relax and allow yourself to experience being nurtured in this way.

**IMPORTANT!** Before you go on with this process, discuss any reservations you have. If you choose not to participate, please stay in the room and be available to be supportive to holders who indicate their needs for help. They may need help in shifting their baby or in getting another pillow, etc. Observe what's going on with one or two partners, so that you'll be in a position to give additional feedback during the sharing.

If you are participating in a Nurturing Exchange and get so uncomfortable that you feel you must stop, do so, and discuss the problem with your partner.

## Doing It

Choose a partner for the first exchange. Do not choose a partner with whom you have or have had a sexual relationship. Decide who will be the holder. Get yourselves settled and follow the Timekeeper's instructions.

About eight minutes after most people have settled into being held, the Timekeeper will say, "Two-minute warning," and the holder will say to the baby, "It's almost time to grow up now." After another two minutes the holder will say to the baby, "It's time to grow up" and the baby will take a few minutes to get reoriented to being a grown-up.

Take a few minutes to write about your experience. After you've completed your writing, share what you've written with your partner. Before switching roles and finding new partners, take a few minutes to stretch and get a drink of water, and then come back and find a new partner so that you can experience the opposite side of the Nurturing Exchange. Repeat the exchange according to the directions of the Timekeeper.

## Between Sessions

Experiment with some of these optional activities.

Read Chapter 10, "Bonding Stage," in *Recovery From Co-dependency: It's Never Too Late To Reclaim Your Childhood.*

Read these books aloud or have someone read them to you:

*When You Were A Baby,* Katharine Ross.
*A Special Kind Of Sister,* Lucia B. Smith.
*My Brother, Will,* Joan Robins.
*Beezus And Ramona* and *Ramona The Brave,* Beverly Cleary.

Get a massage.

Ask for hugs from people you trust, whenever you feel the need.

Take a warm bath and as you bathe, rub soap or oil all over your own body. Take your time, relax and enjoy the experience.

Find a way to observe an infant and appreciate how incredibly wonderful he or she is.

Look for baby pictures of yourself so that you can appreciate how little and innocent you were when you were very young.

Practice some of the activities you discussed about appreciating the essence of another person.

Say to your own Inner Child the things you said to your partner when you were the holder. You may want to use a pillow or stuffed animal to represent your own Inner Child.

Write in your journal.

## Preparation For The Next Session

Bring toys that are suitable for babies who are between one and two years old. Make sure they're large and sturdy so they won't be damaged by babies with grown-up bodies.

Bring stuffed animals, favorite blankets or pieces of fabric that represent favorite blankets. If necessary, bring pillows for comfortably sitting on the floor. Bring books that are suitable to read to a toddler — very simple ones. Label things. Fill only one bag each with toys.

## Closing Song

We will end the meeting with the song "I Love Myself" (p. 40).

# SESSION 7

# ASKING FOR CLOSENESS

As infants, our first developmental task is to bond with our caretakers. As soon as that bond is firmly in place we prepare to break it and establish ourselves as individuals. This preparation occurs between the ages of six months and two years. We prepare to break the bond by exploring our sensory environment and learning what we really want. As we prepare to become separate individuals, we need to make certain that, even when we do what we want to do, our caretakers will be there for us when we need them.

If, to fill their own needs, our parents hold us too close when we're doing this important testing, we may develop a fear of being engulfed. If they let us go too far because they are hurt, distracted or otherwise unavailable for nurturing, we learn to fear abandonment. Most Adult Children are profoundly afraid of both engulfment and abandonment.

In most healthy families, toddlers learn to come and go of their own volition and to trust that their caretakers will be there when needed. In dysfunctional families, children often miss the experiences that allow those learnings. The exercises in this session will allow your Inner Child to experience safety and security while coming close and going away from nurturing — in response to your own inner experience.

71

## SELF-ASSESSMENT QUESTIONNAIRE

Review your responses to items 4 through 7 (pp. 12-13). Scores of eight or above describe skills that people have when they are no longer afraid of engulfment and/or abandonment.

### Worksheet #12: Engulfment And Abandonment

Most Adult Children can identify with the following statements. Read them through and mark the phrases that describe your feelings.

(1) *I'm afraid to get too close to my:*

parent(s)          sibling(s)          spouse          significant other

friend(s)          boss          teacher          subordinate

*If I do, I believe they will:*

leave me      forget me      not wait for me      go away/ignore me

1. Give an example of how this was true for you when you were a child:

_____

_____

2. Give an example of how it is true for you now: _____

_____

(2) *I'm afraid that if I do something I want to do, my:*

parent(s)          sibling(s)          spouse          significant other

friend(s)          boss          teacher          subordinate

*will:*

control me        hurt me        keep me from doing what I want to do

limit me        tell me what to do        hold onto me        trap me

leave me        forget me        not wait for me        go away/ignore me

1. Give an example of how this was true for you when you were a child:

_____

_____

2. Give an example of how it is true for you now: _____

_____

Now give an example of how each of the following statements is true for you:

(3) *I have experienced losing my sense of myself (my own boundaries) when I am in a relationship:* _____

_____

(4) *I have lost a relationship by being myself:* _____

_____

(5) *Others move away when I try to get close to them:* _____

_____

(6) *I move away when someone starts to get close to me:* _____

_____

## SHARING EXERCISE

Share your responses in your small group. Have each person share their answer to question 1 before moving on to question 2, etc.

What could you have done when you were a child when (1) and (2) actually happened?

What would you do now if (1) or (2) actually happened to you? (You may have had it happen and may have done something already. If so, share what you did.)

## Centering Ritual

Ultimately, we need to learn to love and accept all the parts of ourselves. To remind ourselves why, let's sing together "The Greatest Love of All" (p. 15). Form a circle, join hands, and listen carefully to the words of the song as you sing.

When the song is over, return to your seats in your small group area.

## Visualization

*Sit in a comfortable position. Take several deep breaths. Let them out slowly. Now inhale and exhale, and on each inhalation say to yourself "I am . . ." On the exhale, say to yourself, "relaxed." "I am . . . relaxed . . . I am . . . relaxed." Keep repeating this silently.*

Now imagine that you're Jackie. You're 20 months old and you can walk and you can run and you've just learned to climb. You can reach everything on the coffee table and you can reach the things on the edge of the side table, too. Daddy is taking care of you this afternoon and you're having a wonderful time. Daddy is sitting in a chair talking to some big people you don't know. They seem nice, but not very interesting. You go over to Daddy's chair and find a space and wiggle up until you're on the seat and you climb onto Daddy's lap. He puts his arm around you and gives you a hug. You push away and wiggle and say "Down" and Daddy lets you go. You get yourself off the chair, down to the floor.

You walk around the coffee table carefully touching each thing on it and then go back to Daddy's chair. This time you pull yourself up by Daddy's pants and the edge of the chair and climb into his lap again. He smiles and puts his hands on you and picks you up for a hug. You start to wiggle, say "Down," and this time he puts you down on the floor. You walk over to the dog and sit down and hold onto her neck for a minute. Then you go back to Daddy's chair and climb up again.

This time Daddy holds you tight, and you wiggle and say "Down" and Daddy says, "I won't let you go," and you wiggle some more and get loose a little bit. Daddy says, "You're my boy," and you wiggle some more and you say, "Down!" and Daddy puts you down again. Meanwhile Daddy talks to the other big people in the room and you go off again in search of something to do.

You spot Daddy once more and climb up again and again Daddy holds you and hugs you and says, "I've got you this time." You wiggle and wiggle. You push away and Daddy lets go and you wiggle yourself down onto the floor and run away squealing with delight. You're back almost instantly. You climb up again. This time Daddy is deep in conversation with the others. He doesn't pay much attention to you. You climb into his lap, he pats you absentmindedly and you climb down again. You go and play with blocks that are in the corner. You come back over to Daddy, climb back up onto his lap, and snuggle down and sit there, comfortably and contentedly, as he continues to talk to his friends.

Let yourself feel how good it is to be with Daddy, and then, when you're ready, come back to this room and your grown-up body. Open your eyes and stretch.

Sit quietly for a moment or two, then write about your experience. Don't worry about punctuation, capitalization or good grammar. Put the pen to the paper and begin to write. If you missed any part of the visualization, go back and read it in your workbook.

## Group Discussion

Jackie could have learned a lot of things that afternoon. In your small group, discuss whether you think he learned these things and, if so, how he learned them.

Do you think he learned:

- That he and Daddy could want different things, and that he didn't have to want what Daddy wanted?
- To climb more skillfully?
- That he could go away when he wanted to and come back and still get love?
- That grown-ups don't always do what you expect them to do?
- That Daddy would cooperate with what he wanted?
- That it was okay with Daddy for him to do what he wanted to do?
- That he wanted different things at different times?
- That it was safe to do what he wanted to do?

Now share your answers to each of the following questions with other members of your group:

Did you learn the lessons that Jackie learned when you were less than two years old?

- Can you tell someone now, "I don't want to be close to you."
- Can you tell someone now, "I want to be close to you."
- Can you tell someone now when you've had enough closeness, and move away?
- Do you feel comfortable establishing appropriate closeness and distance with other people?
- Do you think you received the kind of responses that Jackie got from his Daddy? If you didn't, what circumstances in your family interfered with your learning that it was safe to come and go when you wanted to, and that you could be in charge of the amount of closeness you received?
- What would you do differently now, if you had learned those lessons before you were two?

## Nurturing Exchange

In the Nurturing Exchange, the roles you will assume are parenter and toddler. The parenters will have some task to do for themselves while supervising their toddlers. Toddlers will play with anything that interests them and come to the parent for nurturing any time they want it. The parent will provide whatever nurturing is needed and allow the toddler to move on when the toddler is ready. The parent may also play games with the toddler like, "I've Got You, You Can't Get Away," making sure that the game is for the enjoyment and learning of the toddler, as well as fun for the parenter.

### INSTRUCTIONS FOR THE PARENTER

Your main job is to provide protection and strokes for your toddler in a way that supports his or her growing independence. You need to be aware of

safety at all times. If your toddler does something that is unsafe, be there to
redirect by offering a safer toy or an alternate way of doing things. At this age,
children may infringe on each other's space or toys, but they are too young to
really know how to share, so if two children want the same thing at the same
time, provide an additional toy or two to distract them.

Toddlers need to learn to take their own initiative to get what they want.
You can offer to read a very simple story book, play ball or demonstrate how
to work a toy. If your toddler is not interested in your agenda, leave the
toddler to her own devices. You can give her a spontaneous hug or pat at any
time. Make frequent eye contact with your toddler and be aware and responsive to what she wants. Avoid hovering.

You may talk with other caretakers about anything that interests you while
staying alert and responsive to the needs of your toddler. You may also
engage in interaction with other toddlers. When your toddler comes to you
for attention, be responsive but not intrusive. When your toddler tries to
leave, either let her go immediately, or playfully invite her to stay a little
longer. Don't insist on your toddler staying. After a while you might try the
game, "You'll Never Get Away," if your toddler enjoys it. Pretend to hold on
to her to keep her from escaping, but after a very brief struggle, let her
escape, so she can feel the power of getting away from a big person.

Give your toddler verbal information and strokes that show that you ap-
prove of her exploring and experimenting and knowing what she wants.
Communicate that you like your toddler and that she is smart and beautiful
and loved. Let her know she can return to you after exploring.

If your toddler cries or acts angry, hug him, comfort him, try to figure out
what's wrong and correct it, or try to distract him with something else
interesting.

When the Timekeeper tells you to, make a game of helping your toddler
pick up the toys and put them away, or at least put them on the side of the
room. At the Timekeeper's signal, tell your toddler it's time to grow up.

### INSTRUCTIONS FOR THE CHILD

Your job is to learn that you can get strokes and attention on your own
initiative and that you do not have to accept attention you don't want. Pay
close attention to how you feel and what you're responding to throughout
this exercise. Act on your feelings. If you want something, go get it. If you
don't want it, leave it, drop it, move on. If you want strokes or attention from
your parenter, go get that.

Let your parenter know what you want. You have some language ability.
You can label many things such as blocks, boxes, babies, food and the names
and sounds of animals. You may be able to speak in short sentences of no

more than five words. You can certainly say "Pick me up," "Rub my head," "Hug," "Play the music," "Open it," "Close it," "Fix it," "Read" and "Cookie." You also show what you want with your body language. It doesn't matter at all to you what your parenter is doing. If you want something, you want it right now.

Notice when you experience enough of anything, whether it's getting your back rubbed, having your hair stroked or playing with a toy. When you experience enough, stop what you're doing and find something else interesting to do. Be sure you make several trips back to your parenter for strokes and attention, so that you have the experience of not being abandoned when you get what you want on your own initiative.

If your parenter plays, "You Can't Get Away," and you enjoy it, go ahead and struggle. If you don't like it or become frightened, sit quietly or cry until your parenter lets you go. When you're invited to help pick up toys, do it if it's appealing to you. If not, do something else that's appealing to you.

When you feel something, express it. When you're angry, act angry, grab things, insist on what you want. When you're scared, go close to your parenter for protection. When you're sad, let yourself cry. When you're happy, laugh or make, happy noises. Take as much time as you need to decide what to do next when you change activities. Rest if you get tired.

**IMPORTANT!** Discuss any reservations you have with people in your group. If you choose not to participate, stay and be available for support. Observe what's going on to give feedback during the sharing.

As always, if you are participating in a Nurturing Exchange and get so uncomfortable that you feel you must stop, do so and discuss the problem with your partner.

## Doing It

Select a partner, follow the instructions of the Timekeeper and proceed with the exchange. When the Timekeeper gives the signal to stop, take a few minutes and write about your experience. After you've written down the important points, share your experience with your partner. When you've each shared, take a break, stretch, get a drink of water and then find a new partner and repeat the exercise from the opposite position.

## Between Sessions

Experiment with some of these optional activities.

Read Chapter 11, "The Exploratory Stage," in *Recovery From Co-dependency: It's Never Too Late To Reclaim Your Childhood.*

Read these books aloud, or have someone read them to you:

*Madeline And The Bad Hat,* Ludwig Bemelmans.
*The Runaway Chick,* Robin Ravilious.
*Curious George Goes Hiking,* Margret and H.A. Reys.
*The Red Balloon,* A. Lamorisse.
*Bears In The Night,* Stan and Jan Berenstain.
*Are You My Mother?,* P. D. Eastman.

Practice extricating yourself from situations in which you feel overwhelmed or engulfed. For example, if you're talking to somebody on the telephone and feel as if you can't get away, interrupt and say, "Excuse me, I need to get off the phone in two minutes" and then do so. If someone is giving you unwanted advice, tell them, "Thank you, I need some time to figure out what I'm going to do," or "Thank you, I've already decided what I'm going to do." If you're watching a boring movie or TV program, turn it off in the middle. If someone else is watching also, find something else to entertain yourself, like reading a book while they're watching. You could even go to another room.

If you're feeling lonely, make contact with a friend. Either call or make arrangements to do something together as soon as you can.

If you feel abandoned by somebody you care about, send them a note or a card asking them to call you, or make direct contact with them and ask them to do something with you. If they say "no" or don't respond, let it go at that. You are no worse off than you were before you made contact. Take the risk that they will respond. You might get what you want if you ask for it.

If you find yourself holding on to a person or experience, notice that you're doing it and discuss with a friend what you might be able to do to detach yourself from the situation or person. Think about the worst thing that could possibly happen to you if you let go. Then think about what you would do if the worst thing really did happen to you.

Ask a friend to go with you to explore a new place, such as a shopping mall, carnival, street fair, market or museum. Arrange to spend part of the time exploring together and part of it exploring separately. Set times during the day to check in with each other to see whether you want to be together or separate. Share your discoveries with each other.

Write in your journal.

## Preparation For The Next Session

Bring children's story books, especially *Where Did I Come From?,* and others from the lists in Sessions 5 or 8, or other books that you loved when you were four or five years old.

Bring hats or costume props for imaginative play. Watch "Sesame Street" at least once. Make a list of at least 20 "Why?" questions that a four-year-old might ask.

## Closing Song

We will end the meeting with the song "I Love Myself" (p. 40).

# SESSION 8

---

# WHY? WHY?
# WHY?

---

Curious preschoolers ask lots of questions because they need information about the world. The ability to ask questions and expect answers is an important skill for any healthy grown-up. Growing up in dysfunctional families, we seldom asked questions, and our question-asking skills are very deficient. We still fear the lack of response, the shame or the ridicule that we got when we asked as children.

When children don't get answers, they create their own. As Adult Children, we pretend to know things that we really have no information about. Many of us live in constant fear that our lack of information will be exposed and we will be seen as frauds. Our Inner Child deserves answers. When we parent each other we need to be honest about what information we have and creative about sharing it on a level a four-year-old child can understand.

## SELF-ASSESSMENT QUESTIONNAIRE

Review your responses to items 14 through 19 (pp. 12-13). These questions represent skills we learn when we are preschoolers.

If you've scored seven or below on any item, this may indicate you experienced a problem during your preschool years.

## Worksheet #13:  Questions

Write down several questions that you think you should be able to answer
but can't, or that you've been pretending you know how to answer. You can
ask about interpersonal relationships, how things work, how people feel or
why things happen. You can even ask about things you wanted to know as
a child but never asked.

(1) _____

(2) _____

(3) _____

(4) _____

(5) _____

### EXERCISE: ASKING QUESTIONS

In this exercise we will be admitting some of the things we have been
pretending to know but really have questions about. We will ask those
questions and respond to each other's questions seriously and respectfully.
Since many of us are so afraid of looking less than perfect, this exercise
takes courage. We can parent each other as grown-ups by honoring the
questioner and the questions. There is no such thing as a dumb question. If
you are curious about something, this is a safe situation in which to ask for
information. If you can't answer a question, please be honest about your
lack of information.

Working in groups of three, ask the first question on your list and get an
answer from either or both of the other members of your group. If no one
knows the answer, discuss where to find the information you want. Now,
have another person ask their question and get an answer. Continue in this
way until you each have had a chance to have all your questions answered
or until the time is up. Take a few minutes to write about your experiences
both asking and answering questions. After you've completed this part of
the exercise, take turns sharing how you felt both asking and answering the
questions.

## Centering Ritual

We need to learn to love and accept all the parts of ourselves. To remind
ourselves why, let's sing together "The Greatest Love of All" (p. 15). Form a
circle, join hands, and listen carefully to the words of the song as you sing.

Return to your small group area.

## Visualization

*Sit in a comfortable position. Take several deep breaths. Let them out slowly. Now inhale and exhale, and on each inhalation say to yourself "I am . . ." On the exhale, say to yourself, "relaxed." "I am . . . relaxed . . . I am . . . relaxed." Keep repeating this silently.*

Imagine that you're Robin. You're four years old and you're very excited because today Mom has left your little brother with a neighbor and she's taking you and a friend to the park to go on the swings and feed the ducks. Mom puts bread in a bag and hands it to you to carry. You point to another loaf and say, "Let's take this, too."

Mom smiles and says, "That's for sandwiches for lunch."

You and your friend put on your jackets and start walking with Mom to the park. You point and say, "There's a flower," and you all stop to look.

Mom says, "It's a crocus."

You walk on and one of the neighbors waves. You wave back. You comment, "He has no hair on top. Why?"

Mom says, "He had some once, but it fell out. Lots of men have hair fall out when they grow up."

You walk on and you get to the stoplight by the school. Mom pushes the button and the light changes. "Why do you have to push the button?" Mom answers, "Not too many cars come here, but to be sure they stop for the children, there is this special button." You walk on, stopping to look at the tiny leaves on a bush.

"Why are they so small?" Mom says, "Because it's spring, and they're just starting to come out. Do you remember how all the old leaves fell off before the winter?" You do remember.

Finally you get to the ducks. You each take some bread and break it into pieces and throw it into the water. The ducks scramble for the bread. Your friend says, "The one with the green head is bigger."

You ask, "Why are they different colors?" Your friend answers, "Because someone painted them," and you giggle. Mom says, "The male ducks and the female ducks look different. The male ducks have green heads and the females are the ones that are speckled brown."

You point to a white one and ask, "What's that?"

Mom says, "That's a different kind of duck, and the males and females are both white."

"Why are they different kinds?"

"I don't know," says Mom, "They just are." Then the bread is all gone. You watch the ducks for a few minutes more. You try to reach them and pet them but they swim away.

As you walk to the playground, you see somebody in a wheelchair.

You point and ask, "Why is he in the wheelchair?" Mom explains that he can't walk and the chair lets him come outside and see what everybody else is seeing.

You say, "Does he have to stay there all the time?"

Mom says, "I don't know. I'm sure he sleeps in a bed like you do, but I don't know whether he stays in the wheelchair at home all the time."

The swings are all full so you and your friend go over to the slide and you each climb up and slide down, and climb up and slide down again. You decide it would be fun to go down headfirst, and start to do it and Mom stops you and says, "No, only feet-first. If your head hit the ground, it might hurt. Feet are meant for bouncing on the ground."

When you get to the bottom, your friend falls down and scrapes her arm. Mom takes her over to the drinking fountain and cleans the scrape with water. She says, "We'll put a Band-Aid on it when we get home."

Your friend asks, "Why do people bleed?"

Mom says, "Everybody has blood inside and skin that covers it up. When the skin gets scraped off, the blood comes out."

Finally you all get to swing. Mom says, "Soon it'll be time to go home."

"Why? I want to stay."

Mom says, "It's almost lunchtime, and I have an appointment this afternoon."

You walk home talking about the ducks. On the way you stop to let your friend go home and to pick up your little brother. Your friend's mother sure looks fat. You ask Mom, "Why is she so fat?"

Mom says, "Because she's growing a baby inside her tummy, like I was before your brother was born."

You say, "Oh," and think about it for a while. Then you say, "Will you read me the baby book again?"

Mom says, "After lunch, when your brother is taking his nap." After lunch, you settle down with Mom on the couch and she reads you the book called *Where Did I Come From?* You giggle at the fat pictures and look at the different body parts that she names. You think about how a Mom and Dad love each other so much that they get close and the Dad gets inside the Mom.

You ask Mom, "Did I start like that?" She assures you that you did. You look at the pictures together of how a baby looks when it's growing and how the Mom's tummy really gets fat. Then you read about the belly button and you look at yours and Mom tickles you and you giggle. You think about what book you want Mom to read next.

Imagining you're Robin, notice how you feel about yourself . . . how you feel about your Mom . . . how you feel about asking, "Why?" When you're ready, open your eyes and come back to the room.

Sit quietly for a moment, then write about your experience. If you missed any part of the visualization, go back and read it in your workbook.

## Group Discussion

Share your answers to these questions in your small groups:

- Did you ask questions when you were small?
- Do you ask questions now?
- Who answered your questions for you?
- Did you learn that it was okay to ask, or did somebody ridicule you because you didn't know the answers already?
- Did someone call you a baby or a nuisance because you wanted to know so much?
- How did you feel about the way Robin's Mom answered her questions?
- Did your caretakers answer your questions to your satisfaction?
- What are some of the questions you didn't dare ask?
- How would you be different now if your questions had been answered differently?

## Nurturing Exchange

In this activity a parenter will be available to answer the questions for the three- to five-year-old. Preschoolers love imaginative play. They put on hats and pretend to be a dancer or a firefighter. They're busy learning about what girls do and what boys do, what men do and what women do. They're very curious about differences between people, including their parents. They are generally satisfied with clear information that is brief and to the point. They do not understand sarcasm and take things very literally. They love to have stories read to them. If they are not "shushed," they have something to say about almost everything.

### INSTRUCTIONS FOR THE PARENTER

It's your job to be available to your preschooler, to answer any questions he might ask and to respond with correct information to any statements he makes that reflect misinformation. For example, a child might say, "Girls can't be firemen." A response to this might be, "You're right. Girls can't be firemen, but women can be firefighters." It's important to respond briefly and clearly with information that is as accurate as possible but simplified to a preschooler's level of understanding.

Preschoolers feel omnipotent, as if they are responsible for all things that happen around them. As a parenter, you need to be alert to your preschooler's misconceptions and clear them up as matter-of-factly as possible. Statements such as, "I made my sister sick," need to be responded to with clarification such as, "Your sister got sick because of a germ. You didn't make her sick. Even if you had the germ first, some people catch germs when other people have them and some people don't."

Children need to be told that they are not responsible for the behavior of grown-ups. If they are not told this, they will assume that they are responsible.

Some children have beliefs such as, "I can stop Daddy from drinking." They need to be told, "Daddy chooses whether or not he will drink and you can't make him decide."

Children may ask hard questions, such as, "What happens to someone when they die?" An appropriate answer might be, "Nobody knows for sure, but I think . . ." When Dad has deserted the family, they may ask, "Where did Daddy go?" Answer truthfully: "Somewhere away from here — I'm not sure where," or "To live in . . ."

Preschoolers need lots of affection and positive affirmation. Hugs and pats are appropriate; at this age they should be offered to the child, rather than imposed upon him or her. Avoid saying, "You're a good child" or "You're a bad child." These labels are inappropriate and confusing. They invite children to worry about being good instead of learning what they need to know.

As a parenter, you can guide the learning of your preschooler. You can do this by offering to read books that cover a particular subject. Be sure to stop and talk about the information in the book, if your child is responsive to invitations to do so. If at all possible, read your preschooler the book *Where Did I Come From?* Sometimes two or three children will gather around one grown-up who's reading. That's fine.

If you don't know the answer to a question your preschooler asks, be honest about not knowing and offer to get the information. Sometimes you can get it from another parenter in the room or speculate aloud with the child on what you think the answer might be.

## INSTRUCTIONS FOR THE CHILD

You are very curious about what people do in the world and why they do what they do. You're also very busy noticing what goes on around you and using your language skills to describe what you see. Say aloud the things you see: "The bear is brown, that lady is fat, there's a kitty, the bird is singing," and so on. Ask the "Why?" questions on the list that you made before this session. Even if your grown-up self knows the answers, ask them from your Inner Child anyway and see how it feels to have them answered respectfully by a grown-up.

Play with toys that interest you. Try on hats. Talk with others about things you like and don't like. Interrupt any time you want to. Ask to have books read to you. Point to the pictures and talk about what you see. Ask any questions the book stimulates. If you don't find out what you want to know, ask again. Ask for any hugs you might want, or any other kind of affection. Talk about things you think you are responsible for, or thought you were responsible for when you were a child. Don't worry about being polite, but don't go out of your way to cause problems, either. If a problem arises out of something you feel like doing, it's your parenter's job to figure out what to do about it.

**IMPORTANT!** If you have any reservations about participating in this exercise, discuss them in your small group. If you choose not to participate, observe participants closely and notice your own feelings in response.

If you are participating in a Nurturing Exchange, and get so uncomfortable that you feel you must stop, do so, and discuss the problem with your partner.

## Doing It

Do the activities described. When the Timekeeper tells you that the activity is complete, tell your preschooler that it's time to grow up. Then each of you spend a few minutes writing about your experience. After you've written about it, share your experience with each other. Take a break for a few minutes. Then find a new partner, switch roles and repeat the activity.

After everyone has completed the activity, clean up the room and put away the toys.

## Between Sessions

Experiment with some of these optional activities.

Read Chapter 14, "Socialization Stage," in *Recovery From Co-dependency: It's Never Too Late To Reclaim Your Childhood*.

Visit a preschool or a playground and observe preschool children. Notice how small and powerless they are. Many Adult Children believe they should have done something different to take charge of their lives when they were only four or five years old. Notice how little impact the will of a small child has on the parenter.

Visit a library or children's bookstore and browse through the books that are recommended for children in the four- to seven-year-old range.

Make an agreement with a friend to ask "four-year-old questions" for a period of time. Ask the friend to follow the instructions for answering questions that were given in the Nurturing Exchange exercise.

Go to the park, swing on a swing, ride a teeter-totter or a merry-go-round.

Keep a list of all the questions that come up for you that you don't ask. Figure out a safe way to ask some of them and get the answers you want.

Ask a friend to take you to the zoo, pretend you're a four-year-old and take care of you and answer your questions.

Have a conversation in fantasy with your own preschool-age Inner Child. Ask your Inner Child what kind of caretaking he or she wants from you right now, and listen for the response. If feasible, find a way to do as the Inner

Child requests. If not, explain to the child why you can't do what's asked and offer something else. Treat your own Inner Child as you treated your partner when you were the parenter.

Read aloud, or have read to you any of the following books:

*Where Did I Come From?,* Peter Mayle.
*The King Who Rained,* Fred Gwynne.
*The Runaway Chick,* Robin Ravilious.
*Alexander And The Terrible, Horrible, No Good, Very Bad Day,* Judith Viorst.
*Amelia Bedelia,* Peggy Parish.
*Dr. Seuss's ABC,* Dr. Seuss.
*My Cat Likes To Hide In Boxes,* Eve Sutton.
*Ten Apples Up On Top,* Theo LeSieg.
*One Fish, Two Fish, Red Fish, Blue Fish,* Dr. Seuss.
*Fox In Sox,* Dr. Seuss.
*Winnie-the-Pooh,* A.A. Milne.

Write in your journal.

## Preparation For The Next Session

Bring the same materials you brought to this session. If you find any additional books you think will be helpful, bring those along. Bring books that talk about responsibility and power and bring ones that give information about setting physical boundaries to protect the child from sexual molestation.

*It's My Body: A Book To Teach Young Children How To Resist Uncomfortable Touch,* Lory Freeman.
*Something Happened To Me,* Phyllis E. Sweet.
*No More Secrets For Me,* Oralee Wachter.

## Closing Song

We will end the meeting with the song "I Love Myself" (p. 40).

# SESSION 9

# JUST HOW POWERFUL AM I?

Many Adult Children spend a lifetime trying to magically control other people's feelings, thoughts and behavior. Others of us believe that other people are in control of our feelings, thoughts and behavior. These beliefs are based on misinformation we received as preschoolers when we were three, four and five years old. As young children, our natural inclination is to think magically. We may believe we're very powerful and can control others, or we may believe that others are very powerful and can control us.

These beliefs are reinforced when our caretakers tell us that people can make each other sick, scared, angry or happy. Learning to sort out who is responsible for what and to understand the difference between thinking, feeling and doing, are important developmental tasks. When we understand these differences, we then understand what we do have power to change and where we are powerless.

Learning these differences helps us make sense of the Serenity Prayer: We need to develop the wisdom to know the difference between the things we can change and the things we cannot change.

## SELF-ASSESSMENT QUESTIONNAIRE

Review your responses to items 15 through 19 (pp. 12-13). These items are associated with successfully giving up the magical thinking characteristic of the preschool years.

If you scored seven or below in any of these areas, you may have had difficulty with understanding what you can and cannot control and in dealing with issues of power and responsibility.

The following Worksheet will help you to examine how some of these beliefs still operate in your life.

### Worksheet #14: Who Makes Whom Feel What?

(1) Mark the statements that you say, think or feel. If you have other favorites, list them under "Other."

_____ He makes me so mad.

_____ She scares me.

_____ You give me a headache.

_____ You make me sick.

_____ You're a good boy/girl.

_____ You hurt my feelings.

_____ She made me laugh/cry.

_____ Other: _____

(2) When you were a child, who made statements like that to you?

_____

(3) List three specific statements they said to you:

1. _____

2. _____

3. _____

(4) What did you say to yourself when those statements were made to you?

1. _____

2. _____

3. _____

(5) Write a statement you use frequently now that is similar to those above:
(Example: My daughter makes me happy.) _____

_____

(6) Now, rewrite your statement in this form: When _____

did to me, I felt _____.
(Example: When *my daughter hugged me*, I felt *happy*.)

_____

(7) Which statement seems more accurate? "My daughter makes me happy" or "When my daughter hugs me, I feel happy"? _____

Why? _____

(8) Which of your statements (in 5 and 6) seems to be more accurate? _____ Why? _____

_____

(9) Do you ever tell yourself that you shouldn't feel a certain way? ____ Yes ____ No (For example: "You shouldn't feel sad that you're leaving an old job because, after all, you're moving to a better job" or "You shouldn't feel bad because another person didn't mean to be hurtful" or "You shouldn't feel bad because you deserve to be hurt.")

What words do you use to tell yourself your feelings are wrong?

_____

(10) Did you ever decide to refuse to exhibit a certain behavior? (Example: Did you once decide that you would never let anyone see you cry?) ____ Yes ____ No
If so, what did you decide? _____

_____

_____

### SHARING EXERCISE

When you've completed your Worksheet, let each person in your small group take one minute to share their own insights.

Then discuss these questions:

• If person A does something, such as yelling an obscenity, and person B responds by feeling angry, sad or scared, is person A responsible for person B's feelings?

- Under what circumstances, if any, can another person make you feel a particular way?
- Can another person force you to keep feeling a particular way? How?
- Can you force another person to think in a particular way? How?
- Can you force another person to behave in a particular way? How?
- Can your feelings have an effect on another person? How?
- Can what you think have an effect on another person? How?
- Can how you behave have an effect on another person? How?

## Centering Ritual

Ultimately, we need to learn to love and accept all the parts of ourselves. To remind ourselves why, let's sing together "The Greatest Love of All" (p. 15). Form a circle, join hands, and listen carefully to the words of the song as you sing.

When the song is over, return to your small group.

## Visualization

When you do this visualization, you will experience being Geri. Geri is four years old and has learned that the way to get what she wants is to whine and cry whenever she has a problem.

Remember that a four-year-old is a very small child. When you're four, you're big enough to open the refrigerator by yourself, but sometimes it's hard to get to places you want to go because you're not big enough or strong enough to move grown-up sized objects, even though you want to. You think you understand how the world works, but sometimes you get confused.

*Sit in a comfortable postion. Take several deep breaths. Let them out slowly. Now inhale and exhale, and on each inhalation say to yourself "I am . . ." On the exhale say to yourself, "relaxed," "I am . . . relaxed . . . I am . . . relaxed." Keep repeating this silently.*

Now imagine that you are Geri. This is a very special day for you. You're visiting Grandma all by yourself. Grandma is busy, and you decide to go out and play. You go to the door and try to open it. It doesn't work. You try again and then you start to cry. Grandma comes over and you tell her tearfully, "I can't get out." Grandma looks down at you and says, "Let's have a talk about feelings." You say, "But I want to get out!" Grandma says, "Come here. When you understand what feelings are for, that will help you get out."

You sit down next to Grandma, and she asks, "Do you know what tears are for?" "No," you sniffle. "Tears are for sad or for hurt. Are you sad? Did you fall down?" "No," you sniffle. "Well, that's what tears are for. If you cry when you feel sad or when you get hurt, you usually feel better. But tears don't work to get the door open. What are you feeling now?" You say,

"I'm mad that the door won't open." "It's okay to be mad," Grandma says, "but if you're mad, will that get the door open?" You start to cry again, "But I *want* the door to open."

Grandma says, "Stop whining. I don't like to listen to you when you whine. What do you think would get the door open?" You say, "I don't know! I'm too little! It won't open!" Grandma says to you, "If you can't get it open, do you know someone who can?" You look at her and say, "You can!" Grandma says, "Are you going to ask me to open it?" And you say with a big smile, "Will you open it for me?" Grandma smiles and says, "Sure. All you have to do is come ask Grandma. Next time you can't get it open, will you come ask me instead of crying and whining?" You nod and say, "Will you open it now?" Grandma does and you go out to play in the sandbox.

Later that day, you want to go out again. You go to the door, try to open it and once again it's stuck. You stand there for a minute and start to cry. Grandma says, "Do you remember how to get the door open?" You look up with a big smile and say, "Will you open it so I can go out?" Grandma does and you go out again.

Later that night, at home with your mom, you tell her, "Grandma says tears are for sad and for hurt, and when I want to go out, I just have to ask."

Imagining you're Geri . . . Notice how competent you feel about getting the door open the first time. Notice how you feel about Grandma at the end of the day . . . how you feel when you're talking to your mom when you're back home.

Let yourself come back to the room and open your eyes. Spend a few minutes writing about your experience as Geri. If you missed any part of the visualization go back and read it in your workbook.

## Group Discussion

A child needs to learn that thoughts and feelings don't make things happen; that people know your thoughts and feelings only if you tell them; that in order to make something happen, you need to *do* something or ask somebody else to *do* something.

Answer the following questions with your small group:

- How did Geri learn these things from her Grandma?
- Do you think Geri will do anything different about other problems after her experience with Grandma?
- How do you think a child learns to believe that crying or whining will get a problem solved?
- How could a child learn that feelings make things happen?
- How could a child learn that neither feelings nor thoughts make things happen?
- How can a child learn what kind of action to take to get something to happen?

- Have you learned to communicate your thoughts and feelings to others?
- Have you learned to choose actions that will help you solve problems?

## Nurturing Exchange

In this exercise, the parenters will set appropriate limits with four-year-olds. The "children" will learn about the impact of their behavior.

### INSTRUCTIONS FOR THE PARENTER

It will be the job of the parenter to maintain safety limits and to respond appropriately to whatever behavior and emotional manipulation the four-year-old presents.

Your job is to set and hold to reasonable limits without shaming, blaming or guilting your charge. **Never** use the following phrases:

- You're bad!
- You're good!
- You make me feel mad (or other feelings)!
- You don't feel that.
- You don't want that.

Making appropriate responses to four-year-olds may feel awkward. Try them anyhow. Label your child's feelings as much as you can: "It looks as if you feel sad . . . It looks as if you feel angry . . . Are you mad? Are you sad?"

If a child says, "But I want to," you can respond, "It's all right to want to, but you're not allowed to do that" or "I know you want to, but you may not do it."

If your child says, "I hate you," you can respond with "It's all right to hate me. I still care about you" or "Are you angry with me because I did something? Tell me what I did that you don't like."

If your child says, "You're a bad Mommy" or "You're bad," say what your name is: "No, I'm Laurie, I'm not bad. You just don't like what I'm doing."

If your child is doing something you feel you must stop, tell them something like: "Stop banging the truck on the wall. It's making marks." If irreparable damage is going to be done to someone or something, say loudly, **"One, two, three, stop!"** Use your best judgment. Resume the activity when you are both ready.

If the child says, "I don't want to," say, "You have to stop, because we're not allowed to make marks on the wall." If a child refuses to stop, say, "If you don't stop, I will take the toy away from you." The child will probably do it again, testing to see if you mean it. If that happens, remove the toy. You then may have a discussion about what they have to do to get it back. The response to this should be to play with it without damaging the toy or anything else. If the child agrees and then uses the toy inappropriately, take it away again with the words, "You agreed not to do that. You may not play with it if you're going to use it the wrong way."

If a child sulks, mopes, has a temper tantrum or cries, say, "You can do that for as long as you want to. It won't get me to do what you want me to do. When you want to talk about what else you can do, come find me and tell me."

If a child tells you how you should feel, tell the child, "I'm responsible for how I feel. I'll like you if I want to like you. You're not in charge of that."

If you need help, don't hesitate to get consultation from others who are in the caretaker role at the same time you are. Remember, there are to be no statements that shame a child in any way, only statements about defining feelings as accurately as you can and statements defining the limits on the child's power. When you set a limit, give a reason for it. ("The toy scratches the paint and it looks messy.") If you feel angry, frustrated or scared, do your best not to act on those feelings. Discuss your feelings when the exercise is complete.

## INSTRUCTIONS FOR THE PRESCHOOLER

In this Nurturing Exchange, you will be a preschool child, about four years old. You will push at reasonable limits, using every form of emotional and physical manipulation that you can conceive of.

You can choose any of the following situations or one of your own. You may choose to imitate a child you know. You may:

- Play more loudly or boisterously than the situation allows.
- Try to convince the parenter that you are starving and should have an ice cream cone or cookies 15 minutes before a meal.
- Ask the parenter to do more things than the parenter is willing to do, such as read three or four books.
- Ask the parenter to let you give a stuffed animal a bath in the sink.
- Try to convince the parenter to let you play in some unacceptable place or with some unacceptable toy.

Some Adult Children feel very frightened about this task. If pushing limits in this way would have led to abuse in your family-of-origin, just push a little bit in this exercise. Try to go slightly beyond your comfort zone. When you were four, you might have been shamed when you tried to do things that made sense to you. If you feel guilty or ashamed when you do these activities, recognize that those feelings are left over from past experiences. Take as much risk as you're willing to take during this exercise.

Start this activity by playing with the toys that are available, reading books if you want to, asking to have them read or playing with other children. When you notice something you would like to do, go ahead and do it, whether or not it is something that is permitted. If you want something that isn't available, tell your parenter. Use any form of emotional or physical manipulation that you can think of to get what you want. **Do not do anything that involves a test of physical strength between you and your parenter.** You may whine, cry, insist loudly, sulk, pout, giggle, hide, threaten — especially silly threats like, "I'm going to turn you into a cookie and eat you" or "I'm going to turn into a snake and slither out of here" or "If you don't, I'll flush you down the toilet" (four-year-olds love toilet talk).

You can also go ahead and do exactly what you were told not to do and see what happens. You can say nasty things to your caretaker, such as "I hate you" or "I won't let you love me" or "You're a bad Mommy (Daddy) (Teacher)." You can do anything at all to try to get your own way. You can refuse to eat or drink. You can hold your breath. You can try to shame your caretaker — anything at all, short of physical violence toward yourself or another person. If you feel like it, you can even lie down on the floor and have a kicking, screaming, temper tantrum. If your parenter tells you, **"One, two, three, stop!"** stop whatever you're doing and discuss the problem before resuming your activity. It is not necessary for you to feel happy or satisfied during this activity, although it is possible to do so.

**IMPORTANT!** If you have any reservations about participating in this exercise, discuss them in your small group. If you choose not to participate, observe participants closely and notice your own feelings in response.

If you are participating in a Nurturing Exchange and get so uncomfortable that you feel you must stop, do so, and discuss the problem with your partner.

## Doing It

Now choose a partner and decide which one of you will be the child. When the Timekeeper gives the signal, proceed with the Nurturing Exchange. When it's time to stop, put the toys away and get the room back in order. Then tell the child, "It's time to grow up now."

Spend a few minutes writing about your experience and share your experience with your partner. Then choose a new partner, review the instructions and repeat the Nurturing Exchange, taking the role you didn't experience earlier.

## Between Sessions

Experiment with some of these optional activities.

Read Chapter 8, "Working with Feelings, Part One," Chapter 14, "Socialization Stage," and Chapter 15, "Working with Feelings, Part Three," in *Recovery From Co-dependency: It's Never Too Late To Reclaim Your Childhood.*

Read *The Magical Years,* by Sonya Freiberg.

Read aloud, or have someone read to you any of the following books:

*Alfie Gets In First,* Shirley Hughes.
*Where The Wild Things Are,* Maurice Sendak.
*The King's Fountain,* Lloyd Alexander.
*Sometimes I Dance Mountains,* Byrd Baylor.
*The Something,* Natalie Babbitt.
*A Big, Fat, Enormous Lie,* Marjorie Wienman Sharmat.
*The King's Flower,* Mitsumas Anno.
*A Summer To Die,* Lois Lowry.
*Ben And Me,* Robert Lawson.
*There's A Nightmare In My Closet,* Mercer Mayer.
*McElligot's Pool,* Dr. Seuss.
*TA For Tots, Volume I and II,* Alvyn M. Freed, Ph.D.
*The Hating Book,* Charlotte Zolotow.
*I Wish That I Had Duck Feet,* Theo LeSieg.
*My Mama Says There Aren't Any Zombies, Ghosts, Vampires, Creatures, Demons, Monsters, Fiends, Goblins Or Things,* Judith Viorst.

Practice making statements that acknowledge your response to another person's behavior, similar to Item 6 on the Worksheet. If you hear yourself make statements blaming someone else for your feelings, restate them to acknowledge your responsibility.

Allow yourself to feel any feelings you may have. Get support from others if you want it.

Make a list of things you haven't allowed yourself to grieve about. Sometimes we try to keep a loss from happening by refusing to feel our grief.

If you're giving up something, even if it's bad for you, allow yourself to feel the loss.

Take yourself someplace where it's safe to play like a child. Go to a children's museum, a zoo, a park and let yourself play like a preschooler.

Make a sandcastle at the beach or in a sandbox. Create a story about what's happening in the castle.

Do something safe but unusual for you. Order a banana split, eat only as much as you want and leave the rest. Play in the mud.

Nurture your own Inner Child the way you parented your partner during the Nurturing Exchange.

Write in your journal.

## Preparation For The Next Session

During the next session, you will be learning or practicing a skill. Bring materials to make a model or do a crafts project that is suitable for a child in grade school. Choose something that you didn't know how to do very well when you were a child, preferably something that you still don't know how to do, but want to learn. You could bring a ball of yarn and knitting needles, a paint-by-numbers kit, a model airplane, a yo-yo or if you don't know how to use one very well, a deck of cards, a hammer, nails and wood, drawing materials, sewing materials, a set of jacks, a bag of marbles or a weaving loom — any of these would be suitable.

## Closing Song

We will end the meeting with the song, "I Love Myself" (p. 40).

# MAKING
# MISTAKES IS OKAY

When you grow up in a family in which there are dire consequences for being less than perfect, the prospect of making mistakes becomes terrifying. It makes sense to decide to pretend you have information that you really lack. When we are expected to know how to do things without ever being shown how, we learn to expect ourselves to do things perfectly the first time, without any help or instruction. We treat ourselves the way we were treated.

During this session we'll have experiences to help us learn that making mistakes is okay, and that we can learn from our mistakes.

## SELF-ASSESSMENT QUESTIONNAIRE

Review your responses to items 20 through 22 (p. 13). These are related to learning from mistakes. Scoring seven or below on any of these items indicates you may need additional experience in this area.

Even though you may pretend to others that you don't make mistakes, everybody who is alive makes mistakes.

## Worksheet #15: Mistakes

(Adapted from *Recovery From Co-dependency: It's Never Too Late To Reclaim Your Childhood,* p. 74.) Think about a mistake you've made recently, whether or not anyone else knows that it was a mistake.

(1) Give an example of a mistake that you have made: _____

_____

(2) What did you learn from the mistake? _____

_____

(3) Did you know that before? _____

(4) Were you doing the best you could with the information you had?

_____

(5) What problems were created when the mistake was made? _____

_____

(6) How have you corrected the problems that were created by the mistake? _____

(7) Would you forgive someone else who made that mistake? _____

(8) Will you forgive yourself for your mistake? _____

1. If not, why not? _____

2. If not, what is the alternative? _____

(9) When you were a child, what happened when you made mistakes?

_____

(10) When that happened, what did you decide about yourself and other people? _____

(11) How does what you learned about mistakes as a child affect you now? _____

### SHARING EXERCISE

When you've completed the Worksheet, discuss the results in your small group. Let each person take a minute or two to describe their mistake, what they've learned from it, what problem it caused, how they fixed it and whether or not they've forgiven themselves. Remember to be supportive of other people.

After each person has had a chance to talk about their recent mistake, share what happened when you made mistakes when you were a child and how that affects you now (answers 9, 10 and 11).

## Centering Ritual

Ultimately, we need to learn to love and accept all the parts of ourselves. To remind ourselves why, let's sing together "The Greatest Love of All" (p. 15). Form a circle, join hands, and listen carefully to the words of the song as you sing.

When the song is over, return to your small group area.

## Visualization

This visualization is a little different. Instead of a single episode, you will be Ronnie and imagine what it's like at three different times in your life.

Ronnie has a very special mother who was shamed a lot when she was a little girl. She is determined to treat Ronnie differently from the way she was treated, so he can learn from his mistakes.

*Sit in a comfortable position. Take several deep breaths. Let them out slowly. Now inhale and exhale, and on each inhalation say to yourself "I am . . ." On the exhale, say to yourself, "relaxed." "I am . . . relaxed . . . I am . . . relaxed." Keep repeating this silently.*

You're Ronnie, and you're two-and-a-half years old. You're not very big at all, but you have your own crayons and you love to color. One day you take your crayons out and start to color on the kitchen table. Your mother says matter-of-factly, "Tables are not for coloring on. You can get paper or a coloring book and color on that." Then she says, "Let's clean these marks off," and she gives you a sponge to rub on the table. You do some, and then she takes over and finishes. You get a coloring book and color.

On another day, when you're a lot bigger — you're three-and-a-half now — you're going shopping with Mom. Instead of riding in the cart, you're walking alongside. You're very busy looking at all the things in the grocery store. You see the cereal that you've seen on the cartoon shows. Suddenly you notice that you have to go to the bathroom. You tell Mom, and she says, "Okay," and turns the cart around, but by the time you get to the end of the aisle, you can't hold it anymore. You stand there feeling just terrible as the wet, warm liquid runs down your leg and makes a puddle on the floor. Mom says, "That's too bad. Let's take care of these groceries and go right home."

She takes you home, washes you, changes your clothes and says, "Don't worry about it, you just waited a little too long to tell me. Tell me a little sooner next time. I know that you can keep your pants dry."

Another day, long after this, when you're big enough to go to school, you're six years old and you're in first grade. Yesterday, Mom and Dad told you that today's a very special day. It's their tenth anniversary, and they're going to sleep late. You decide that because it's such a special day, you're going to do something very special: You're going to make them breakfast. You've never done it before, but you've watched Mom make scrambled eggs lots of times, and you're sure you can. You are allowed to use the microwave to heat up hot dogs, so you know how that works.

You carefully climb on a chair and take the eggs out of the refrigerator and put them on the kitchen counter. Then you move the chair and get a bowl out of the cabinet to break the eggs into, just like you've seen Mom do. You bang an egg on the edge of the bowl just like you've seen Mom do. When she does it, the egg cracks and she takes both hands and separates it. When you do it, the egg smashes and half the egg and shell goes into the bowl and the other half goes onto the counter. Uh oh! Now what? You pick the eggshell out of the bowl, or at least all that you can get. You try to scoop the egg from the counter into the bowl. That doesn't work very well, so you take the sponge and push the mess into the sink.

Then you take another egg and try again. This time the whole thing falls into the bowl and you have to pick out the shell again. You pick out most of the pieces. The next egg goes partly in the bowl, partly on the counter and partly on the floor. You sigh, clean it up again and decide you better put one more egg in the bowl. It breaks and only a little shell gets into the bowl. You decide to leave it that way, and stir it up and put it in the microwave. You cook it until you can see through the door that it's beginning to puff up. So you turn off the microwave and decide to make toast to go with the egg. You take the bread out of the bag and put it in the toaster.

Then you remember that they like coffee. You're not allowed to use the stove, so you turn on the water until it gets very hot and you put a big spoonful of instant coffee into each cup and fill it with water from the tap. You then put plates and coffee and eggs and toast on the table and proudly go wake up Mom and Dad and tell them that breakfast is ready. A few minutes later they come into the kitchen and look around; then they sit down and start to eat. Mom says, "I think we better put this back in the microwave for a little bit" and heats things up. Mom tastes the eggs and they crunch. She says to you, "I don't really like scrambled eggs with shells in them. I don't think I want to eat these, but I appreciate your thinking about us and making them for us."

Dad tells you, "Thank you very much for helping us celebrate our special day" and reminds you that your favorite cartoon show is on. You go in the family room to watch TV and see the end of your show. When you come back, they're drinking coffee and cleaning up the kitchen.

Mom says, "I think you need some egg-breaking lessons. Let's make more eggs for all of us." She says, "When you're first learning how to break eggs it's not easy, so you break them over a cup instead of a bowl. It also works well to tap them with the edge of a knife instead of trying to hit them on the side of a bowl. After the egg is broken into the cup, you can use a spoon to take out any eggshell, and then put the egg into the bowl." She shows you how to do it, and you practice and get all the egg into the cup, and then you proudly empty the cup into the bowl.

Mom puts the rest of the stuff into the bowl and lets you stir it around. Then she pours it into a pan and puts it into the microwave. Later that day she tells you, "I know you wanted to do something special for us, making breakfast, but I don't think you're quite big enough for that yet. Next time you want to cook, tell me and I'll help you. We'll practice making breakfast together before you do it alone again."

Imagining you're Ronnie . . . Notice how you feel when you're three-and-a-half, and Mom talks to you about keeping yourself dry after she changes your clothes. Notice how you feel when you keep making messes as you break the eggs by yourself . . . how you feel about Mom not wanting to eat your eggs. Notice how you feel when you break the egg with Mom's help.

Now begin to come back to this room. When you're ready, open your eyes. Spend a few minutes writing about your experience. If you missed any part of the visualization, review it now in your workbook.

## Group Discussion

Discuss the answers to the following questions with your small group.

When he made mistakes, Ronnie learned that they created problems that had to be solved.

- What problem had to be solved when he was two-and-a-half?
- How did that problem get solved?
- How do you think Ronnie felt when he solved the problem when he was two-and-a-half?
- What problem had to be solved when he was three-and-a-half?
- How did that problem get solved?
- How do you think Ronnie felt when Mom solved the problem when he was three-and-a-half?
- What problem had to be solved when he was six?
- How did that problem get solved?
- How do you think Ronnie felt when he solved the problem when he was six?
- What do you think Ronnie will do when he makes mistakes in the future?
- How do you think he will feel when he makes mistakes in the future?
- What did you learn about mistakes when you were a child?
- Did anybody show you how to fix them?

- What do you do now when you realize you have made a mistake?
- How do you feel?

## Nurturing Exchange

One of the main activities during the grade-school years, ages six through 12, is learning how to do various tasks. During these years we learn to read, write, spell, make things, play games, do arithmetic and interact with our peers.

We learn these skills most effectively when we can try them out, see how they work and get help from people who are already skilled in the tasks we need to learn.

In this Nurturing Exchange you will learn or practice a skill you would like to have and you will teach someone something at which you are already skilled. In this process you will be encouraged to learn from your mistakes.

In this exercise the parenter and the child become the teacher and the learner.

### INSTRUCTIONS FOR THE TEACHER

It's your job to help the learner learn. If you are very skilled at something but have never taught someone else to do it, you may be very surprised at what simple tasks a learner needs to master. You may need to break the skill into small segments, rather than trying to teach the whole process at one time. If you're teaching somebody to sew, you may teach them first how to thread a needle or how to put a pin into a piece of fabric. If you're teaching someone to play a musical instrument, you may have to teach them how to hold it before you can teach them how to play it.

One of the most effective ways to help somebody learn is to allow them to explore and experiment on their own before you teach them what works best for you in a particular skill area. Be sensitive to the needs of your student. Some people prefer to be shown in detail first, while others prefer to explore first.

For this project, forget about the right way to do something and help your student learn a way that works for herself or himself.

Avoid using any words that might encourage the learners to feel bad about themselves. Instead of saying "That's wrong," say, "If you do it that way, this is what I think will happen. Do you want to try it and see, or do you want to try a different way?" Ask questions like, "Does that feel comfortable for you? What do you think will happen if you do it that way? Which way works most comfortably?" Feel free to make suggestions about other options, but if they are rejected, don't insist that the learner follow your program.

Send "I" messages: "When I play jacks . . ." Avoid the word "should." Listen to your learner's feedback and use it to guide your teaching.

Remember, your learner is just beginning to explore an activity that you might be an expert at. She or he may be doing it just to see how it feels. Your ideas about how important it is to do it a particular way may not match your learner's agenda. Be responsive to what your learner needs, rather than insisting that the learner be responsive to your approach.

Pay attention to what you learn by teaching. Acknowledge the learner for trying things even if they don't work out very well.

If the learner becomes discouraged, try encouraging her by sharing stories of mistakes you made when you were learning the skill. Let the learner decide when to stop. If the learner asks for additional instruction after the exercise, decide whether or not to provide that instruction, based on your own needs, feelings and available time. You are not required to continue this exercise beyond the time allotted. (This might be a good opportunity to practice your 'no-saying' skills!)

## INSTRUCTIONS FOR THE LEARNER

Your job is to learn something new, while acting as if you are a child in grade school. Choose an age between six and 12 and tell your teacher how old you will be. Tell your teacher what you want to learn and how you want to be helped.

Decide whether you want your teacher to show you first how to do the task, or whether you want to experiment and ask for help only when you need it.

As you are learning, decide how much you want to learn about it. If your teacher says you could do better, either keep learning or say, "I've done as well as I want to." Sometimes you learn something and like it so much you want to keep doing it and learn even more about it. Sometimes you learn how to do something and discover that you don't like doing it and that you would like to stop as soon as you can. If you want to hammer a nail into a block of wood, you don't have to build a birdhouse just because someone else thinks it's a good idea.

Sometimes it's not fun to do something until you've practiced enough to be good at it. If your teacher tells you that something will be more fun with practice, use the information to help decide about whether to continue.

If your teacher is going too quickly or too slowly for you, or you feel frightened, angry or sad while you're learning, stop and talk about the problem before you continue the learning process.

If you get started on something and would like to continue past the time allotted, negotiate with your teacher for additional time after the session.

Your teacher may agree, but is under no obligation to continue after the session is over.

**IMPORTANT!** If you have any reservations about participating in this exercise, discuss them in your small group. If you choose not to participate, observe participants closely and notice your own feelings in response.

If you are participating in a Nurturing Exchange and get so uncomfortable that you feel you must stop, do so, and discuss the problem with your partner.

## Doing It

Each of you will tell the entire group what skill you would like to learn using materials you brought with you: "I would like to learn to (knit, build a model airplane, work a yo-yo, play jacks, etc.)." If you can teach a skill someone else wants to learn, raise your hand so the learner knows you would make a suitable partner.

Divide the group into learners and teachers. Learners find a partner who can teach you what you want to learn. The teacher is a resource for the learner. The learner needs to be responsible for his or her own learning. One teacher may assist more than one learner simultaneously. You may have the opportunity to learn more than one skill during this session.

Find a comfortable place for the teaching/learning experience and get started. When the time is up, spend a few minutes writing about your experience and then share your experience with your partner. Switch roles, let the new learners find partners who will help them learn what they want to know and repeat the process.

Return to your small group and share your answers to the following questions:

- How is this learning experience different from learning experiences you've had in the past?
- How is this teaching experience different from teaching experiences you've had in the past?
- Share one thing that you learned by making a mistake and correcting it.

## Between Sessions

Experiment with some of these optional activities.

Read Chapter 16, "Latency Stage," in *Recovery From Co-dependency: It's Never Too Late To Reclaim Your Childhood.*

Read some of the following books:

*I'm Terrific,* Marjorie Wienman Sharmat.
*Charlie And The Chocolate Factory,* Roald Dahl.

*Louis Braille: The Boy Who Invented Books For The Blind,* Margaret Davidson.
*It's So Nice To Have A Wolf Around The House,* Harry Allard.
*Carlos Goes To School,* Eloise A. Anderson.
*Paddington's Garden,* Michael Bond.
*Helen Keller,* Margaret Davidson.
*A Twister Of Twists, A Tangler Of Tongues,* Alvin Schwartz.
*Nobody Is Perfick,* Bernard Waber.

Get a catalog from an adult education facility in your community and mark classes that interest you. Sign up for a class if you want to. You can drop out at any time after you've learned what you want to know.

Ask a friend to teach you something you've been trying to figure out on your own. (I once asked a neighbor to teach me how to make pie crust.)

Get help to complete a project you've been leaving undone because you're stuck.

Throw away a project that you were going to finish someday because you were supposed to and not because you wanted to.

Try doing something at which you were once skilled, but are now out of practice. Do it just for the fun of it.

Keep track of the mistakes you make and what you learn from each of them.

Risk doing something new that you don't know how to do yet.

When you make a mistake, admit it to another person and tell them what you've learned.

When you're learning a skill, treat your Inner Child the way you treated your partner in the Nurturing Exchange.

Write in your journal.

## Preparation For The Next Session

No supplies are needed.

## Closing Song

We will end the meeting with the song, "I Love Myself" (p. 40).

# SESSION 11

# NEGOTIATION SKILLS

Many Adult Children of dysfunctional families may spend their whole lives avoiding conflict. Conflict may make us uneasy or even terrify us, depending on our experience with conflict when we were children. When faced with conflict, we may quickly give in and placate our opponent or we may strive to win at any cost. We rarely attempt to negotiate, because we haven't learned the negotiation skills that children see modeled in healthy families.

Conflict is natural when people live together or associate with each other. What each of us wants and needs at any given time differs from the wants and needs of others. We need ways to solve the problems created by those differences.

Under ideal circumstances we learn to resolve the conflict in a win-win way that takes the needs of all parties into consideration. Grade-school children in healthy families spend years practicing arguing with their parents and their peers in an attempt to resolve those differences. Conflict is an opportunity to negotiate or argue for your point of view. If you grew up in a dysfunctional family, you may believe that the only outcome of an argument is that one person wins and others lose. You may believe that might makes right or that conflict is dangerous. You need to learn the techniques of win-win negotiation by practicing with others.

## SELF-ASSESSMENT QUESTIONNAIRE

Review your responses to items 23 through 25 (p. 13). These items refer to skills developed by grown-ups who practiced win-win arguments in childhood. If your response to these items is seven or below, you probably need additional work on your negotiation skills.

Now take a few minutes to complete Worksheet #16.

## Worksheet #16: Conflict

Mark all that apply:

(1) I sometimes avoid conflict by:

_____ Pretending not to notice it.
_____ Giving in automatically.
_____ Saying I will do what is wanted and then not doing it.

_____ Other: _____

(2) When I'm in a conflict situation, I usually:

_____ Try to talk longer, louder and faster than the other person.
_____ Try to listen to their point of view.
      Actively ask questions about their needs.
_____ Talk about my own needs.
_____ Get antagonistic and demanding.
_____ Give in and give up.
_____ Compromise (give up some of what I want if the other gives up something).
_____ Get help.

_____ Other: _____

(3) When I disagree with someone, I behave as if the most important outcome for me is:

_____ To have the other person like me.
_____ To win.
_____ To lose.
_____ To keep them from winning.
_____ That we are both satisfied.

_____ Other: _____

(4) How are the answers to #3 different if the conflict is with:

    1. An authority figure _____

    2. A peer _____

    3. A subordinate _____

(5) Describe what you usually do when someone hints to you that they would like you to do something you don't want to do:

    1. An authority figure _____

    2. A peer _____

    3. A subordinate _____

(6) Describe what you usually do when someone tries to change an agreement with you and you don't want to change it:

    1. An authority figure _____

    2. A peer _____

    3. A subordinate _____

(7) Describe what you usually do when you've made an agreement you

    don't want to keep: _____

(8) How did your important caretakers handle conflict?

    1. Mother _____

    2. Father _____

    3. Other _____

(9) How would you like to change the way you respond to conflict now?

_____

## SHARING EXERCISE

Briefly share your answers to questions one through eight in your small group. Spend some time discussing question nine in your group.

## Centering Ritual

Ultimately, we need to learn to love and accept all the part of ourselves. To remind ourselves why, let's sing together "The Greatest Love of All"

(p. 15). Form a circle, join hands, and listen carefully to the words of the song as you sing.

Return to your small group area.

## Visualization

In this visualization, you'll experience what it's like for 11-year-old Chris to practice successfully the negotiation skills she's been learning for the last five or six years.

*Sit in a comfortable position. Take several deep breaths. Let them out slowly. Now inhale and exhale, and on each inhalation say to yourself "I am . . ." On the exhale, say to yourself, "relaxed." "I am . . . relaxed . . . I am . . . relaxed." Keep repeating this silently.*

Now imagine that you're Chris. You're 11, you live with your mom and your stepdad and your half-brother and sister who are six and four years old. It's summer vacation, and you have an agreement with Mom that she'll pay you for spending two hours every day supervising the younger children — reading them stories, taking them to the park or just hanging out with them. It's 9 o'clock in the morning. You're about to leave for the park with the little kids when a friend calls and asks if you can spend the morning with her at the pool at her apartment complex and then have lunch and go to a movie in the afternoon. The idea sounds wonderful, but you have an agreement to take care of the kids. You say you'll ask your mom and call back in a few minutes.

When you ask Mom she says, "No, I need you to take care of the kids. I have work I have to get done for one of my clients and it's due this afternoon. You can go to the movie this afternoon, but you can't go to the pool. I need your help, and you agreed to give it to me."

You really want to go swimming. You ask Mom if it's okay if you take care of the kids at the pool instead of the park. She's a little leery and asks, "Are you sure it would be okay with your friend?" Mom knows there's a lifeguard at the pool and a wading pool for little kids. You call your friend back and explain the situation and ask her if she'll help take care of the kids if you come over and keep her company at the pool. She agrees. You go tell your mom.

Then you tell your mom that it's too far to walk. "I could get there on my bike, but it's too far for the little kids to go. Would you drive us over and pick them up at 12:30?" Mom says, "I can't do that. I have to meet with my client and give her the report at 12:30. Why don't you pack a picnic and I'll pick up the little kids at 1:00." You protest, "But then we won't have time to get to the movie."

Mom gets a little exasperated and says, "Well, if you stay here, then I can take you over there, pick up your friend and take you both to the movie after I meet with my client." You think about that idea, but you really want to go swimming, so you ask, "Well, if we went to the second show I wouldn't be able to be home in time for supper. Could I swim, come home late, miss supper with the family and just make my own?" Mom says it's okay. You call your friend and ask her if she can go to the second show instead of the early one. She checks, her mom says yes, and asks if you would like to stay for dinner at her house. Your mom gives you permission to do that. You help the little kids get their things ready to go swimming.

As Chris, notice how you feel now that you have figured out a way to do what you want to do and still keep your agreement to help your mom. Now bring yourself back to this room and this time. When you're ready, open your eyes and spend a few minutes writing about your experience as Chris. If you missed any part of the visualization, take time to reread it in your workbook now.

## Group Discussion

In your small group, discuss these questions:

- What are the choices that Chris could have made when her friend first asked her to change her plans?
- What are the choices she could have made when her mother first said no?
- What were her options when her mother couldn't take charge of the children until it was too late to make the early show?
- Do you think Chris understood her mother's point of view?
- Do you think her mother was satisfied with the outcome?
- Do you think the younger children were satisfied?

Chris and her mother are successful win-win negotiators. Chris knew what she wanted and what her mother wanted. She learned the reasons why her mother wanted something different from what she wanted. She was able to figure out a way to do what she wanted while satisfying her mother.

- What did you learn about negotiation when you were growing up?
- What kinds of things happened in your family when you tried to negotiate?
- In your family-of-origin, who won negotiations? Who lost?
- Are you a successful negotiator now?
- What skills do you need in order to become as successful as Chris?

## Nurturing Exchange

In the Nurturing Exchange, the child will choose one of the following situations and the parent will negotiate with the child until a solution is reached. The solution must take into account the needs and wants of both the parent and the child and the resources available in the situation:

*Situation 1:* A 10-year-old wants to spend the night at a friend's house. The parent believes the supervision there may be inadequate.

*Situation 2:* An 8-year-old's bicycle is stolen because he didn't put it away. He wants the parent to purchase a new one.

*Situation 3:* A 9-year-old refuses to wear her new shoes because they are not the latest style.

*Situation 4:* At the end of the first marking period, an 11-year-old, who has been telling her parents that she has no homework, brings home a report card with bad grades and a notation that she hasn't been turning in her homework.

*Situation 5:* A 6-year-old wants to stay up an hour past bedtime on a school night to watch a special TV show.

*Situation 6:* A 10-year-old wants to go to a rock concert with three other 10-year-olds.

*Situation 7:* Your choice: perhaps something you have needed to resolve with your own children.

## INSTRUCTIONS FOR THE PARENTER

Your goal is to teach your child win-win negotiation skills. In order to do that you need to model what you want the child to learn. You may not use force or coercion to achieve the outcome you want. You are not to give in to the child's position against your better judgment. When negotiating, stay focused on providing a positive outcome for both of you. Focus on the problem to be solved, not on the characteristics of the person. Ask questions to help clarify exactly what the child wants. Try to find out why that particular want or result is important to the child.

Listen actively. Summarize each statement the child makes before responding to it. Tell the child your goal in the situation and the reason for your goal. Avoid blaming, name-calling or shaming your child. Search for a creative solution which lets both of you achieve your goals. Help your child learn these win-win strategies by modeling them and repeatedly inviting the child to participate in them.

## INSTRUCTIONS FOR THE CHILD

Do your best to get the outcome you want, using whatever reasons you can think of to argue for your own position. Typical school-children's arguments are: Everyone else is doing it. It won't hurt me. I really want to. If I don't, something terrible will happen to me. You're a bad parent if you don't give me what I want. I can handle it. It won't cause a problem. I'll feel bad if I don't get my way. My friends will think I'm a baby. Giving me what I want will prove that you love me. I'll hate you if you don't give me what I want.

You must stay and complete the negotiation until you and your parenter are both satisfied or until time runs out.

**IMPORTANT!** If you have any reservations about participating in this exercise, discuss them in your small group. If you choose not to participate, observe particpants closely and notice your own feelings in response.

If you are participating in a Nurturing Exchange and get so uncomfortable that you feel you must stop, do so, and discuss the problem with your partner.

## Doing It

Begin your negotiation at the direction of the Timekeeper. If you finish before the allotted time, take a new situation and work with that. When you've completed the first part of the Nurturing Exchange, take a few minutes to write about your experience and then share it with your partner. Then, find a new partner, take the opposite position, reread the instructions and repeat the nurturing process.

## Between Sessions

Experiment with some of these optional activities.

Decide what skills you will need to practice between sessions, in order to meet your goals.

Read Chapter 16, "Latency Stage," in *Recovery From Co-dependency: It's Never Too Late To Reclaim Your Childhood.*

Read *Getting to Yes: Negotiating Agreement Without Giving In,* by Roger Fisher and William Urey.

Read any of the following books that are favorites of grade school children:

*Iggy's House,* Judy Blume.
*Eli,* Bill Peet.
*The Magic Well,* Piero Ventura.
*Mr. Popper's Penguins,* Richard Atwater.
*The Lorax,* Dr. Seuss.
*Yertle The Turtle,* Dr. Seuss.
*Can You Sue Your Parents For Malpractice?,* Paula Danziger.

Initiate a negotiation with someone about a problem you've been avoiding discussing.

Create an agreement to barter goods or services with a friend.

Negotiate which restaurant to go to with a friend.

Negotiate with someone to give you a discount on goods or services.

Prepare to ask for a raise. List all the reasons why you think you deserve it and all the reasons why giving you a raise would be of benefit to your employer. List all the reasons that your employer might have for not wanting you to have the raise at this time. Make a decision about whether to actually ask for the raise.

Negotiate with your boss or your spouse for a day off.

Negotiate with a police officer to park in an illegal zone for a period of time.

Negotiate with friends to treat you as if you were king or queen for a day.

Write in your journal.

## Preparation For The Next Session

Make a list of ten things you would like to have in your life that you don't have now and that other people might be able to provide for you or help you find.

Make a list of ten things that you could provide for others, either free or for an appropriate reciprocal exchange. Bring these lists to the next session with you.

## Closing Song

We will end the meeting with the song "I Love Myself" (p. 40).

# SESSION 12

# MORE ABOUT BOUNDARIES

Webster's Dictionary defines a boundary as "that which indicates or fixes a limit." Boundaries are a critical issue for Adult Children of dysfunctional families. Since most of us grew up in situations in which boundaries between people were defined either too rigidly or too loosely, most of us are very uncertain about how to set boundaries in our current lives. We let ourselves get so involved with others that we lose our sense of ourselves. We sometimes limit our contacts with others so severely that we feel isolated and alone. We can't seem to find a middle position.

In this session, we will examine our beliefs about boundaries in various situations. Then we will practice learning to negotiate appropriate boundaries for ourselves and those with whom we relate.

## SELF-ASSESSMENT QUESTIONNAIRE

Look at how you filled out the Self-Assessment Questionnaire during Session 3 (pp. 12-13). If any of your answers have changed, indicate the changed answers to items 8, 9, 10, 17, 23, 24 and 25 now.

Any response at level seven or below probably indicates a need for additional work on boundaries.

## Worksheet #17: Boundaries

(1) A friend calls at four a.m. and says, "I'm having trouble sleeping. I
keep wondering whether or not to tell my parents how angry I am at
them."
How do you *feel?*

      Sad     Mad     Glad     Scared     Other _____

What do you think you *should* do? _____

How *do* you act or behave? _____

(2) You see someone from this group in a grocery store. She looks like
she's been crying.
How do you *feel?*

      Sad     Mad     Glad     Scared     Other _____

What do you think you *should* do? _____

How *do* you act or behave? _____

(3) You are in a minor automobile accident 30 miles from home. Your car
is disabled. There's no public transportation and you know your
spouse/best friend/significant other is involved in completing a major
project with a deadline.
How do you *feel?*

      Sad     Mad     Glad     Scared     Other _____

What do you think you *should* do? _____

How *do* you act or behave? _____

(4) At a party, an acquaintance greets you with a wet kiss and overly tight
hug.
How do you *feel?*

      Sad     Mad     Glad     Scared     Other _____

What do you think you *should* do? _____

How *do* you act or behave? _____

(5) You're out hiking in the country. You see a beautiful lake in the
distance. As you get closer, you discover there's a fence around it.
How do you *feel?*

      Sad     Mad     Glad     Scared     Other _____

What do you think you *should* do? _____

How *do* you act or behave? _____

(6) You are allergic to cigarette smoke. At work, someone you don't know lights a cigarette near you in a no-smoking area.
How do you *feel?*

      Sad     Mad     Glad     Scared     Other _____

What do you think you *should* do? _____

How *do* you act or behave? _____

### SHARING EXERCISE

When you have completed this Worksheet, share your responses in your small group. There are no right answers in any of these situations. The object of the sharing is to find out what your limits are and how they are like or unlike other people's limits. This will give you more information and suggest areas in which change is possible.

Discuss each person's responses to one situation before you go on to the next situation.

## Centering Ritual

Ultimately, we need to learn to love and accept all the parts of ourselves. To remind ourselves why, let's sing together "The Greatest Love of All" (p. 15). Form a circle, join hands, and listen carefully to the words of the song as you sing.

Return to your small group area.

## Visualization

*Sit in a comfortable poistion. Take several deep breaths. Let them out slowly. Now inhale and exhale, and on each inhalation say to yourself "I am . . ." On the exhale say to yourself, "relaxed." "I am . . . relaxed . . . I am . . . relaxed." Keep repeating this silently.*

Now imagine that you're Tony. You're 13 years old and in the 8th grade. Your mom died two years ago and you live with your dad and older sister. You get reasonably good grades and pretty much do what's expected of you in school. You really love video games and bicycles. You and your friends are getting interested in girls, and you've managed to acquire a few copies of *Playboy,* which you've hidden safely away in your room. You come home from school, and you're met by your outraged father.

He says, "I went into your room when I needed my hammer and screw-driver and couldn't find them where they belonged. I could barely get through the door. There's stuff everywhere, including the four forks that I haven't been able to find and that you swore you knew nothing about. I found pop cans that are half full, dirty plates and your clean and dirty clothes all over the floor. I don't know how you tell what's clean and what's dirty. You agreed to keep your room clean, and I agreed to stay out of there. You also agreed to put family things back where they belong, like my tools and the things that go in the kitchen. You're not keeping your end of the bargain, and I'm so angry I feel like going in with a shovel, cleaning it out myself and going in every day to make sure you keep it that way. I want you to tell me today when you're going to get it clean, and what kind of inspection system we're going to set up. I'm not willing to have a health hazard in my house."

You feel angry and scared, and immediately react defensively: "What right did you have to go into my room? You promised to stay out. I was going to clean it tomorrow. I didn't mean to take your stuff, I just forgot to put it back. I needed it for a project. Besides, I know where everything is, and there is a path to the door."

Dad repeats, "You haven't kept the agreement you made. If you want private space, you have to be responsible for it. I'm not going to talk to you anymore about it now. Let's both cool off. Go up and do your homework, and we'll talk about it after dinner."

You hurry to your room and carefully check to be sure the *Playboy* magazines are exactly where you left them. They are. You fume for a while about how Dad is always bugging you, and how when you grow up and have a place of your own you'll keep it exactly how you want it. And how you do too know where the clean clothes and dirty clothes are. Finally you put on some music and think about how you're going to manage this one. You pull out the paper where you'd written down your agreements, which you and Dad both signed. It said you'd clean your room every week, that you wouldn't bring food into the room unless you cleaned up the food debris immediately after you ate and that he would leave your stuff strictly alone if you kept those agreements. You think about how much you don't want anyone messing with your stuff. You knew what was going to happen and you messed up. You decide you'd better get things cleared up by renewing your agreement. The last thing in the world you want is for your dad to be in charge of cleaning your room. You decide that you'll add to the agreement that he can inspect it once a week if you're there. You pile up the dirty dishes and silverware and carry them into the kitchen with you. You bring down the agreement, too, and tell your dad, "I don't want you in my room. I'll take care of it. I'll clean it on Saturday, and you can come in and inspect, and then I'll clean it once a week and you can inspect it if I'm there."

Dad says, "Okay, but if my stuff is missing and I know you've been using it, I'll still go in to get it if I need it, even if you're not there." You don't like this, but you decide you can live with it, and that you'll be very careful not to leave any family stuff in your room. Dad says, "Thank you. I really didn't want to be responsible for your things. I know you're big enough to handle it yourself." He reminds you that if you want your laundry done with the family wash you need to bring it to the washing machine and he'll leave your clean clothes outside your door. That sounds good to you and you dig into dinner.

Imagining you're Tony . . . Are you surprised at your dad's confrontation when you arrive home from school? Why haven't you kept your agreement up until now? Notice how you feel when you're thinking about what to do. Notice how you feel when you go down and tell your dad about your new proposal.

Now slowly come back to this room, in this time and in this place. Take a few minutes and write about your experience as Tony and what you learned. If you missed any part of the visualization, read through it in your workbook now.

## Group Discussion

Discuss the answers to the following questions with your group:

- Do you think Tony's dad violated his boundaries by going into his room?
- Do you think Tony violated his dad's boundaries? How?
- Do you think Tony's dad was being fair with him? Do you think he would have carried out his threat?
- Do you agree with Tony's decision?
- Do you think he'll carry it out?
- Did you have any private space when you were Tony's age?
- What did you need to do to protect your own space?
- Do you have any private space now?
- What do you need to do to protect it from others?
- Do you have any private time now? Can anybody interrupt you at any time?
- Do you always answer your telephone?
- How can you protect your own time now?
- Do you feel as if you're doing an adequate job of communicating your boundaries to others?
- What changes do you want to make?

## Nurturing Exchange

In this Nurturing Exchange you will practice negotiating agreements. These can be agreements that you didn't have the opportunity to negotiate when you actually were an adolescent, or they can be agreements you'd like to negotiate with some individual in your current life.

As adults we must constantly negotiate agreements that indicate our limits to others. We need to negotiate agreements about limits on time, about public and private space, about physical touch, about sex, about using automobiles, about owning and caring for animals, about chores, about money and about attention that we need and want from others. You may choose your practice negotiations from any of those areas.

Your partner will role play fhe individual with whom the agreement is to be negotiated.

Think about a time in the past or in your life now, when boundaries were or are unclear. If you have difficulty coming up with your own situations, the following examples may remind you of opportunities for negotiation:

- A professional woman discovers that her newly acquired 12- and 14-year-old stepsons prefer to watch television in her bedroom because "It's the most comfortable place in the house."
- One spouse keeps promising to be home with the car so the other spouse can use it and keeps breaking the time agreements.
- An adolescent with a job buys things he especially likes, and his brothers and sisters appropriate them, use them indiscriminately and break them.
- An aging mother calls her adult son five to ten times a day at his business.
- A neighbor repeatedly borrows garden tools and sometimes returns them damaged.
- A friend borrows your car and returns it with the gas tank almost empty. You are late to work because you need to stop and get gas and haven't allowed extra time.
- Items on the list you created between sessions.

Answer the following questions before you proceed, and share all of this information with your negotiating partner.

- Is the situation from the past or the present?
- Who is involved?
- What is or was the situation?
- What outcome do you want to achieve?
- Has the other person involved demonstrated any awareness of your need for limits or boundaries?
- Do you believe they will negotiate with you or be outraged at the idea of your wanting your own boundaries?

If you can't find a situation of your own in which you want to practice establishing boundaries through negotiation, choose one of the sample situations.

## INSTRUCTIONS FOR THE BOUNDARY SETTERS

Tell your negotiating partner about the situation in which you want to negotiate boundaries. Give your partner as much information as possible about the person he or she is to role play. Be sure to tell your partner whether he or she is role-playing a cooperative or uncooperative negotiator. Ask your partner to take whatever role you need for your greatest growth and learning.

Use the following guidelines for effective negotiation: State what the problem is for you, why it is a problem for you and what outcome you would like to achieve. Ask your role-playing partner what outcome she or he would like to achieve and why. Suggest as many options as you can think of that would help you get the result you want. Ask your negotiating partner if she or he can see other options. Try to reach agreement. If you do, write out your agreement. Be sure to include who will do what, and when. Now, negotiate the penalty clause: What will each of you do if you do not honor all aspects of the agreement that you've made? Write this down too. When you are done, each of you sign the agreement.

If you are not able to reach an agreement, add the following step: Think about what you will do if you do not reach an agreement. Ultimatum is one strategy; resignation and/or surrender is another. An ultimatum should be used only if all else fails. Ultimatums sometimes come out sounding like threats. Be certain not to make a threat you are not willing to carry out. Examples:

- If you don't come for counseling, I will leave this relationship.
- If you return the car with no gas in it, you may not use it again for a month.
- If you keep going into my room without permission, I'm going to put a lock on my door.
- If you keep making sexually inappropriate remarks, I'll file suit for sexual harassment.

Your negotiating partner does not have to agree to this statement. It's a statement of your boundaries, your limits and what you are going to do if another person refuses to honor them.

The best negotiated settlements always take into account the needs of both participants, the feelings of both participants and what the resources of the situation allow.

## INSTRUCTIONS FOR THE ROLE-PLAY PARTNER

Listen carefully to the scenario and to the description of the character you are to play. Ask as many questions as you need to in order to thoroughly understand your role. When you are role-playing, do your best to take on the character you're being asked to play, even if that character does things very differently from the way you would like to do them.

Don't concede any points just to be nice. As you negotiate, take the needs and the feelings of the character you're playing into account. Work assertively to have those needs and feelings acknowledged in the negotiation.

Play your role enthusiastically, so that your partner can truly test his or her negotiating skills. Be sure the negotiation addresses the needs and feelings of both of you and what is possible to achieve in the situation. It's all right not to reach a settlement.

Check frequently with your partner about whether you are role-playing effectively.

If you receive an ultimatum, stay in your role and tell your partner what you will do in response to it.

**IMPORTANT!** If you have any reservations about participating in this exercise, discuss them in your small group. If you choose not to participate, observe participants closely and notice your own feelings in response.

If you are participating in a Nurturing Exchange and get so uncomfortable that you feel you must stop, do so, and discuss the problem with your partner.

## Doing It

Now go ahead and negotiate. If you finish with one situation, you might try to do another one, until the time limit is reached. Follow the instructions of the Timekeeper.

When you've completed your negotiation, take a few minutes to write about your experience. Share your experience with your partner. Take a break and find a new partner. Review the instructions. Take the opposite role and repeat the exchange.

## Between Sessions

Experiment with some of these optional activities.

Read Chapter 15, "Working With Feelings, Part Three," and Chapter 17, "Adolescence," in *Recovery From Co-dependency: It's Never Too Late to Reclaim Your Childhood.*

Read *Getting To Yes* by Roger Fisher and William Urey.

Make a list: of any time you feel your boundaries have been violated; of situations in which you are not certain how to treat someone else's boundaries; of situations where you think what you want to do would violate someone else's boundaries. Discuss these lists with a friend.

Negotiate with someone about establishing or changing a boundary.

Talk to someone concerning what you want done about an agreement she or he has broken with you.

Play a game of Monopoly.

If you make a purchase that is unsatisfactory, return it to the store where you bought it. If you order a meal in a restaurant that is incorrectly prepared, send it back to have it corrected.

Ask someone to turn down music that is too loud.

Refuse to talk with a telephone solicitor. Tell them you never buy things over the telephone. Buy a telephone answering machine. Use your telephone answering machine to screen your calls before you talk to anyone.

Ask someone to open or close a window or otherwise adjust the temperature of a room in which you are uncomfortable.

Read any of the following books:

*The Phantom Tollbooth,* Norton Juster.
*Ruby The Red Knight,* Amy Aitken.
*From The Mixed-up Files Of Mrs. Basil E. Frankweiler,* E.L. Konigsburg.
*Chicano Girl,* Hila Colman.
*What Mary Jo Wanted,* Janice May Udry.
*Princess Penelope's 365 Dresses,* Mariette Vanhalewijn.
*Cat In The Hat,* Dr. Seuss.
*Fish Is Fish,* Leo Lionni.
*Mrs. Piggle Wiggle* series, Betty MacDonald.
(In addition, review the reading list from Session 3.)

Write in your journal.

## Preparation For The Next Session

Keep a record of times during the week when you're aware of your Inner Child. Carry an index card with you in your purse or pocket, and anytime your Inner Child shows up, please make a note of it. Bring your card to the next session.

## Closing Song

We will end the meeting with the song "I Love Myself" (p. 40).

# SESSION 13

## PARENTING YOUR OWN INNER CHILD

The goal of this program is to develop a healthy Inner Parent that can take care of your own Inner Child. To take care of your Inner Child, you need to recognize the signs that indicate your Inner Child needs something.

Sometimes it's easy. We know our Inner Child is present when we go into a stressful situation and suddenly discover that we're feeling as if we were a little kid and wish we had somebody to take care of us or someplace to hide. This phenomenon, known as *automatic spontaneous age regression,* is unmistakable. As we learn the techniques we've practiced in this program, we can switch our awareness to the part of us that knows how to respond to that Inner Child and provide appropriate nurturing for ourselves.

We will use this session to develop that dual awareness: the awareness that the Inner Child is present and the awareness that there is more to us than that. We now know that we also have healthy functional grown-up parts we can use to take care of that needy little person within us.

You have probably already been doing this. There have been times during the last weeks when you've been upset about something and almost automatically calmed yourself.

You can learn to be alert to the needs of your Inner Child by recognizing your own personal cues — your signals that the child is needy. Sometimes a strong emotional response, stronger than the situation seems to call for, indicates the existence of left-over childhood emotions which are still in need of attention. Fears of being abandoned or of being too close to another person usually refer to unresolved childhood experiences. Urges to engage in addictive or compulsive behaviors usually indicate the Inner Child's need for some sort of parenting.

As you become more alert to these signals and learn to respond to them, you become a better and better parent to your own Inner Child.

## SELF-ASSESSMENT QUESTIONNAIRE

Complete this new copy of the Self-Assessment Questionnaire. Be as accurate as you can. Your answers may or may not have changed since you started the program. This copy of the questionnaire shows the age range of a child learning these skills. Responses of seven or below at any age usually indicate that your Inner Child of that age is especially vulnerable. When you are trying to figure out the age and needs of your Inner Child, think about the ages where you have the fewest skills (lowest ratings). Often those Inner Children are the ones who need the most parenting.

**BONDING STAGE** (Birth to 6 to 9 months)

|  | Never | Seldom | Sometimes | Often | Always |
|---|---|---|---|---|---|
| 1. I know when my body needs something (food, air, water, rest, etc). | 1  2  3 | 4  5 | 6  7 | 8 | 9  10 |
| 2. I am effective about making sure my environment supports my physical needs. | 1  2  3 | 4  5 | 6  7 | 8 | 9  10 |
| 3. I know when I need strokes. | 1  2  3 | 4  5 | 6  7 | 8 | 9  10 |

**EXPLORATORY STAGE** (6 to 9 months to 18 to 24 months)

| | | | | | |
|---|---|---|---|---|---|
| 4. I am comfortable in new situations. | 1  2  3 | 4  5 | 6  7 | 8 | 9  10 |
| 5. I can try out new things without getting in trouble or hurting myself. | 1  2  3 | 4  5 | 6  7 | 8 | 9  10 |
| 6. I am comfortable selecting what I like and don't like in new situations. | 1  2  3 | 4  5 | 6  7 | 8 | 9  10 |
| 7. I can enjoy myself by exploring something new. | 1  2  3 | 4  5 | 6  7 | 8 | 9  10 |

|  | Never | Seldom | Sometimes | Often | Always |
|---|---|---|---|---|---|

SEPARATION STAGE (18 to 24 months to 30 to 36 months)

8. I feel independent and autonomous.  1  2  3  4  5  6  7  8  9  10

9. When I make decisions, I count  1  2  3  4  5  6  7  8  9  10
myself and others equally.

10. I am comfortable sharing my ideas  1  2  3  4  5  6  7  8  9  10
and opinions with others who have
ideas of their own, even if their
ideas differ from mine.

11. I am comfortable about the ways in  1  2  3  4  5  6  7  8  9  10
which I am different from others.

12. I am comfortable about the ways in  1  2  3  4  5  6  7  8  9  10
which I am similar to others.

13. I am able to be vocal and stubborn  1  2  3  4  5  6  7  8  9  10
in opposing things I think are
destructive.

SOCIALIZATION STAGE (3 to 5 years)

14. I am comfortable asking questions  1  2  3  4  5  6  7  8  9  10
when I don't understand or want to
know something.

15. I can recognize and acknowledge  1  2  3  4  5  6  7  8  9  10
other people's feelings.

16. I have the ability to find out what  1  2  3  4  5  6  7  8  9  10
others feel when I don't know.

17. I can confront others when I see  1  2  3  4  5  6  7  8  9  10
problems in what they are doing,
saying or feeling.

18. I can tell when to give up on  1  2  3  4  5  6  7  8  9  10
something that isn't working.

19. I am willing to feel sadness and  1  2  3  4  5  6  7  8  9  10
grief when I have to let go of some-
thing that was important to me.

LATENCY STAGE (6 to 12 years)

20. I am comfortable learning how to  1  2  3  4  5  6  7  8  9  10
do new things that I didn't know
how to do before.

|  | Never | Seldom | Sometimes | Often | Always |
|---|---|---|---|---|---|

21. I do things as well as they need to be done.  1 2 3 4 5 6 7 8 9 10

22. I finish things that need to be finished.  1 2 3 4 5 6 7 8 9 10

23. I can recognize and communicate about the reasons for my values and beliefs.  1 2 3 4 5 6 7 8 9 10

24. I can recognize and understand that others have different reasons for their values and beliefs.  1 2 3 4 5 6 7 8 9 10

25. I am comfortable negotiating openly with others to satisfy our needs and wants.  1 2 3 4 5 6 7 8 9 10

**ADOLESCENT STAGE** (13 to adult)

26. I recognize and am comfortable with the fact that I am connected to other people.  1 2 3 4 5 6 7 8 9 10

27. I can be interdependent with others without sacrificing my own autonomy.  1 2 3 4 5 6 7 8 9 10

## Worksheet #18: Caring For Your Inner Child

Think of three different situations in which your Inner Child needed something in the past week. Answer these questions for each situation:

What happened? _____

_____

_____

_____

Who were you with? _____

_____

_____

What did your Inner Child need? _____

_____

_____

_____

What did you do about it? _____

_____

_____

_____

If you had it to do over again, what, if anything, would you do differently?

_____

_____

_____

_____

Now list three to five ways in which you are nurturing your own Inner Child differently since you started this program:

1. _____

2. _____

3. _____

4. _____

5. _____

### SHARING EXERCISE

When you've completed this Worksheet, share your answers in your small group. Be sure to acknowledge each other for the changes you've been making.

## Centering Ritual

Ultimately, we need to learn to love and accept all the parts of ourselves. To remind ourselves why, let's sing together "The Greatest Love of All" (p. 15). Form a circle, join hands, and listen carefully to the words of the song as you sing. When the song is done, return to your seats.

## Visualization

In this visualization, instead of being another child, you will be your own Inner Child. You will also be your grown-up self, with all of the health and growth you've acquired in your lifetime.

You will have several opportunities for the current you to practice nurturing your child within. In some areas, nurturing will be easy; in others, it will be more difficult. This is a learning experience, not a final exam. Simply notice how you respond and how you feel about your responses.

*Sit in a comfortable position. Take several deep breaths. Let them out slowly. Now inhale and exhale, and on each inhalation say to yourself "I am . . ." On the exhale, say to yourself, "relaxed." "I am . . . relaxed . . . I am . . . relaxed." Keep repeating this silently.*

> Let your grown-up self travel back through time until you find a familiar place; you recognize the place where you lived when you were a brand new baby. Your grown-up self is invisible to any other grown-ups you may encounter, so feel free to move around. Look around the dwelling. See who else is there. See what arrangements have been made for this precious new being. As you encounter the baby, the baby you once were, let your consciousness merge into the consciousness of the baby and notice how you feel. Are you comfortable and happy . . . safe and warm . . . or are you frightened and alone . . . or desperate? Experience the world from the consciousness of your infant self for a moment or two.
>
> Now, with your grown-up self, take your baby self in your grown-up arms. Hold the baby close to you and notice how you feel as a grown-up and how you feel as a baby, as you tell your infant self, "I'm so glad you're here. I'm so glad you were born. You belong in this world. You are wonderful. I love you. I'll always be with you if you need me. You can count on me to take care of you. You're wonderful and perfect just the way you are. It's all right for you to need things and I'll be happy to respond to your needs." Hold the baby close.
>
> Add any more messages you have. As the baby, be aware of how you feel, being held by you, the grown-up. As the grown-up, be aware of how you feel holding and nurturing the baby, your infant self. Be together for a little while. When you're comfortable and satisfied, put the baby down and say goodbye for now. Look around once more and leave.
>
> Now, move forward through time until you find your childhood home, the home of your two-year-old Inner Child. Go in and look around. See who else is there. Are the people there happy? Are they frightened or angry or sad? Whom do you see? What are they doing? Look through the house until you find your two-year-old self. Notice that your two-year-old self is having a hard time. You want something, and somebody else is not allowing you to have it. What's more, you're supposed to be doing something that

you don't want to do. Let your grown-up consciousness merge with the consciousness of what it's like to be two and feeling very frustrated.

Shift your awareness back to your grown-up self. What can you do to help your frustrated little two-year-old? Finally you decide; you go over and take the two-year-old in your lap. You sympathize with the two-year-old and tell your child that you know he or she is getting big and can do lots of things. You tell your child, "You're learning how to think for yourself. It's okay to know what you want and what you don't want. It's okay not to want to do things, but sometimes you have to anyhow. I love you no matter what you do. And I love you no matter what you don't do. I know you'll find a way. You're a smart little child. It's okay for you to feel however you feel. And it's okay to know what you know. I love you. And you can come to me whenever you need to. I'll always be here for you."

Now sit and rock and hug your two-year-old and say anything else you want him or her to know about. Shift your awareness back into your two-year-old Inner Child. Notice how you feel being hugged and rocked and talked to by your grown-up self. When your grown-up self is ready, release your two-year-old self. Take a last look around and leave. Know that you can come back whenever necessary.

Now let yourself drift on in time for about two years. Go to the place where your four-year-old Inner Child is living. Once again, look around, See who's there. Notice the atmosphere. How do people feel? Are they happy? Are they sad? Are they afraid or angry? What activities are going on? Wander around until you find your four-year-old child self huddled on a bed, feeling very unhappy. Now shift your consciousness so that you are aware of all the feelings of your unhappy four-year-old child self. Shift back to your grown-up awareness and sit down on the bed next to the child.

Stroke the child gently and ask "What's wrong?" Now shift your awareness again, and, as the child, feel the gentle touch of the grown-up self from the future, and answer the question. Tell why you're so unhappy. Talk about what kind of attention you need that you're not getting, what you don't understand or how sad you are that someone important to you isn't here for you anymore. Talk to your grown-up self and feel the touching and the caring. As the grown-up, listen carefully to your four-year-old child, and answer her or him as honestly and clearly as you can. If your child will allow it, hug your child and carry on the conversation that she or he needs to have with a loving grown-up. Be sure to tell your child self that you love her or him. Tell your child that he or she is a fine, okay little boy or girl, and that if there are problems, you'll be there to help work them out. Reassure your child that he or she does not make bad things happen in the world, but when uncomfortable things happen, you as a grown-up can help. Let your conversation go on for a few more minutes. Set up a signal system with your four-year-old Inner Child so that she or he can get your attention whenever it is needed. When you're ready, open your eyes and let yourself return to this room.

Spend a few minutes writing about your experience of nurturing your own Inner Child. If you missed any part of this visualization, read the text in your workbook.

## Group Discussion

Discuss these questions with your small group:

- What age Inner Child was it easiest for you to nurture?
- Why?
- What age was more difficult for you to nurture?
- Why do you think this is true?
- Did your Inner Child believe that you would be able to be a resource to him or her?
- As the child, how did you feel in response to the self-nurturing?
- Was it easier to receive nurturing at one age than another?
- What skills do you still need to develop to be able to nurture your Inner Child effectively?

## Nurturing Exchange

This Nurturing Exchange will help you enhance the dual awareness of your Inner Child and of your grown-up self. You can learn to provide appropriate parenting and support for the child you once were and still are.

This Nurturing Exchange will take place between your grown-up self and your child self. Your partner will support you by listening carefully as you nurture yourself aloud and by making suggestions to help keep the exchange flowing.

During the self-nurturing exercise, you will be the Nurturing Parent to your Inner Child, and give her or him what is needed to solve the problem. If the problem cannot be solved, you will help your Inner Child to feel better, and give him or her resources to use in the future.

To help you prepare for this self-nurturing exercise, take a few minutes to complete the following Worksheet.

## Worksheet #19: Emotions — Windows To Your Past

(1) Describe a time recently when you had an emotional response that seemed out of proportion to the current situation. If you can, let

yourself feel that emotion now. _____

_____

(2) Go back in time and think of a time when you felt that emotion when you were in high school. _____

_____

(3) If you can, take it back even further and remember a time when you felt that emotion when you were in grade school. _____

_____

(4) Going back further yet, remember a time when you felt that emotion and you hadn't yet started school. _____

_____

(5) What is the earliest time you can remember feeling that emotion?

_____

(6) What was going on? _____

_____

(7) What kind of parenting or support did your child need at that time?

_____

   If you had difficulty answering Questions 1 to 7, answer the following questions instead:

(8) Think of a time when you were a child and needed nurturing that you didn't get. What was going on? _____

_____

(9) What kind of parenting or support did you need at that time? _____

_____

## INSTRUCTIONS FOR THE SELF-PARENTER

Sit in a chair, facing an empty chair. In the empty chair, imagine the child you once were, who needs nurturing now. You may be able to visualize how s/he looks, what s/he's wearing and what posture s/he's assuming. If you can't visualize those things, just imagine them in any way you can and proceed with the instructions. Look at the child and say, "I know that you're unhappy. Will you tell me about the problem?" Then change seats.

Sit in the child's seat and respond to the grown-up who is nurturing you. Say whatever comes to mind. Let your body assume whatever position is comfortable for the child. Do your best to assume the persona of the child. When you've completed your response, which may be lengthy or just a few words, switch chairs and be the grown-up again. As the grown-up, respond to what the child has just told you. Switch back and forth as feels appropriate, until you've reached some sort of resolution.

When your observer/supporter makes comments and suggestions, follow them if they feel right to you. Ignore them if they seem to be interfering with the natural flow of the experience.

## INSTRUCTIONS FOR THE OBSERVER/SUPPORTER

You are the witness to the self-nurturing experience. Pay close attention to the words being said and the body language, as your partner moves from chair to chair. If you observe that your partner has missed responding to something that was said, call it to his or her attention, such as: "Your child said that she was scared, and you didn't respond to that." If you see incongruities between the words being said and the body language, report that to your partner.

For example, "You said you were okay while in the child's seat, but you were all hunched over and still looked terrified." Your partner may or may not respond to your observations and suggestions. Tune into your own intuitions.

If it feels right, suggest that your partner say something again louder, or put into words the emotion that his or her body seems to be expressing. For example, have your partner say, "I'm angry!" when he looks angry but hasn't verbalized it yet. When your partner appears to be finished, ask him to say one more thing.

If your partner appears to be stuck and going nowhere, except repeating the same things over and over again, ask whether it seems as if it might be a good place to stop.

**IMPORTANT!** If you have any reservations about participating in this exercise, discuss them in your small group. If you choose not to participate, observe participants closely and notice your own feelings in response. Some people are not comfortable with the dual role-playing process. If you like, you can substitute a written dialogue for the spoken dialogue between your grown-up self and your Inner Child. If you choose this option, please follow the instructions for the Alternative Nurturing Exchange.

As always, if you are participating in a Nurturing Exchange and get so uncomfortable that you feel you must stop, do so and discuss the problem with your partner.

## Alternative Nurturing Exchange

Write a dialogue between your grown-up self and your Inner Child. As your grown-up self, write with your accustomed hand and, when your Inner Child responds, use your non-accustomed hand to write the response.

If you are the partner to a person working in this way, you can do an extra nurturing experience for yourself by creating a written dialogue between your own Inner Child and your current grown-up self.

When you're both finished writing, share as you would after an ordinary exchange.

## Doing It

Begin the self-nurturing experience at the direction of the Timekeeper. When the Timekeeper signals the end of the exercise, write for a few minutes about your experience in each role, and then share your experience with your partner. Find a different partner, and repeat the self-nurturing exercise in the opposite role.

## Between Sessions

Experiment with some of these optional activities.

Read the following chapters in *Recovery From Co-dependency: It's Never Too Late To Reclaim Your Childhood:* Chapter 7, "The Treatment Environment," (which describes how to create a safe environment for an Inner Child); Chapter 8, "Working With Feelings, Part 1" and Chapter 9, "Diagnosing Developmental Dysfunctions: How Old is the Inner Child?"

Read any of the following children's books:

*The Little Engine That Could,* Walter Piper.
*Island Of Blue Dolphins,* Scott O'Dell.
*Charlotte's Web,* E.B. White.
*Necessary Parties,* Barbara Dana.
*The Day The Senior Class Got Married,* Gloria Miklowitz.
*Rock Star,* James Lincoln Collier.
*Hunches In Bunches,* Dr. Seuss.

Practice noticing when your Inner Child appears. Whenever your Inner Child shows up, spend a few minutes figuring out how old he or she is and what he or she needs.

Repeat the Nurturing Exchange exercises from this program either physically or in fantasy.

Create a wish list: Whenever you have a thought about wanting something or wishing you had it, write it down on the list.

Choose something to do each day which is nurturing for your Inner Child, and do it.

Read *Wishcraft* by Barbara Sher. Go to an adult education class and learn to do something new.

Stop at a park and play on the playground equipment. Watch a Walt Disney movie just for the fun of it.

Take your Inner Child to the circus, the zoo or some other wonderful place.

Write in your journal.

## Preparation For The Next Session

Compare your answers on the Self-Assessment Questionnaire with the goals you set for yourself at the beginning of this program. Congratulate yourself on your progress. Remember, this is just a beginning.

Make a list of all the people in your life now who can be supportive to you. Bring the list and a crayon or fiber-tip pen to the next session.

## Closing Song

We will end the meeting with the song, "I Love Myself" (p. 40).

# SESSION 14

## LEAVING HOME

The goal of parenting is to help the child learn the life skills that are necessary to function competently in the world. To prepare the child to leave home and to function well without parents, we need a healthy Inner Parent who assures us it's okay and important for us to take good care of ourselves. We need an Inner Parent to remind us that other people's needs are important, too. We need an Inner Parent to remind us to negotiate when our needs seem to conflict with those of others.

When your Inner Parent functions in this way, most of your responses on the Self-Assessment Questionnaire will be at level eight or above.

This program has helped you learn to use your Inner Parent to care for your own Inner Child. You can now acknowledge and care for some needs of your Inner Child yourself. If you grew up in a very difficult family situation, you most certainly need more parenting than this program was able to provide. This session will help you find appropriate help to care for your Inner Child when that's necessary.

You probably need additional help in specific areas. You can clarify the specific help you need by checking the lower scores on your Self-Assessment

Questionnaire. Your response to each Nurturing Exchange can also direct you to your own incomplete developmental tasks. If you wish that a particular exchange could be repeated again and again, you can arrange to get help and repeat it.

Many people need to be physically held, touched and nurtured repeatedly over a long period of time, before they experience that the hole inside is filled. Others need extensive practice in saying no and learning to count themselves as well as others. Some of us need a good deal of information about the world and an extended opportunity to ask questions and get clear answers.

Now that you've learned to identify what you need and to parent each other, it's time to identify the resources you and others can exchange to help your Inner Child continue to grow.

## SELF-ASSESSMENT QUESTIONNAIRE

Review the Self-Assessment Questionnaire (pp. 128-130). What are the developmental areas where your Inner Child is still looking for additional parenting in order to develop the competencies listed? Each developmental stage is labeled on the questionnaire, so you can identify which stage needs additional work. The sessions of the program that addressed the developmental tasks of each stage are listed here:

**Bonding Stage: Birth to 6-9 months**
    Session 5: Learning to Ask
    Session 6: Holding and Touching

**Exploratory Stage: 6-9 months to 18-24 months**
    Session 4: I Don't Know What I Want
    Session 5: Learning to Ask
    Session 7: Asking For Closeness

**Separation Stage: 18-24 months to 30-36 months**
    Session 3: Creating Boundaries
    Session 12: More About Boundaries

**Socialization Stage: 3 to 5 years**
    Session 8: Why? Why? Why?
    Session 9: Just How Powerful Am I?

**Latency Stage: 6 to 12 years**
    Session 10: Making Mistakes is Okay
    Session 11: Negotiation Skills

**Adolescence: 13 to adult years**
    Session 12: More About Boundaries
    Session 13: Parenting Your Own Inner Child
    Session 14: Leaving Home

## Worksheet #20:  Your Personal Network

Your personal network includes all of the people you know and others to whom you have easy access. It includes people in this program. A list of names of people who are supportive of you is probably the most important network resource you have. Use the list you made between sessions to help complete this Worksheet. You may not be able to list people in all these categories yet.

(1) List people who admire you and affirm your success: _____

_____

(2) List people who give you valuable information: _____

_____

(3) List people who help you get things done: _____

_____

(4) List people who support you when you're having emotional diffi-

culty: _____

(5) List people who could help you negotiate for a major purchase like

a house or a car: _____

(6) List people from whom you could get physical nurturing: _____

_____

(7) List people who would help you explore new things that interest you:

_____

(8) List people with whom you could negotiate to test your boundaries:

_____

(9) List people who test your boundaries whether you want them to or not. For example:

- Someone who interrupts you and talks longer than you want to on the tele-

phone: _____

- Someone who tells you what to do when you haven't asked: _____

_____

- Someone who gets angry with you when you don't meet his or her unspoken

expectations: _____

(10) List people with whom you can ask silly or personal questions about things you think you're already supposed to know: _____

_____

(11) List people who teach you how to do things: _____

_____

(12) List people with whom you most like to play: _____

_____

(13) List people to whom you feel you are closest: _____

_____

### IDENTIFYING SUPPORT EXERCISE

When you've completed the list, answer these questions in your small group:

- Do I have the support system I need in my life now?
- What are the areas in which I need more support?
- Do I think I'm giving enough, too much or not enough support to others?
- Do I have the support I need to help me fill in the gaps on my Self-Assessment Questionnaire? If not, how can I get that support?

## Centering Ritual

Ultimately, we need to learn to love and accept all the parts of ourselves. To remind ourselves why, let's sing together "The Greatest Love of All" (p. 15). Form a circle, join hands, and listen carefully to the words of the song as you sing.

When the song is done, return to your small group area.

## Visualization

A prayer begins: "Birth is the beginning, and death a destination . . . life is a sacred pilgrimage — to life everlasting." (*Gates Of Repentance, The New Union Prayer Book For The Days Of Awe;* Central Conference of American Rabbis; New York; 1978.)

To help affirm your life and to put this period of recovery into perspective, this final visualization asks you to look at your life by imagining that you are very old, your life is complete and you are reviewing the steps of your journey. You will imagine your life *after* recovery. Completing your recovery does not mean you will never again have to think about recovery. It simply means that the focus of your attention and your life shifts to doing other things. The skills and lessons you've learned during recovery become automatic and no longer need your undivided attention.

*Sit in a comfortable position. Take several deep breaths. Let them out slowly. Now inhale and exhale, and on each inhalation say to yourself "I am . . ." On the exhale, say to yourself, "relaxed." "I am . . . relaxed . . . I am . . . relaxed." Keep repeating this silently.*

Now imagine that you are very, very, very old. You know that this is the last day of your life. It's the last day of a very fulfilling, rewarding, productive life.

Since you are about to release these experiences and let your spirit move on, you wish to review once more the events that have brought you to this place and time.

Think back to your childhood and briefly remember the rewards and the losses, the joy and the pain, that created the foundation of who you have eventually come to be. Remember the struggles of your adolescence, the paths you took that were dead ends and those that were productive. You recall the challenges you experienced as a teenager. (Pause one minute.)

As you review the events in your life, the ones that helped shape who you are today stand out. These were the challenges of your 20s, your 30s, your 40s, your 50s, your 60s and your later years. (Pause one minute.)

You remember how, so long ago, you started the process of *recovery.* What an interesting word to use. From this perspective, the recovery process was just one more step, a very important step, bringing you toward this day, so many years later, at the very end of your life.

You remember how this process became the foundation of so many of the joyful and fulfilling events that were to come later.

You remember the recovery process as a time of great struggle and great reward. You recall how you got started. Who helped you? Who supported you? Who sponsored and encouraged you to learn what you needed to learn? (Pause one minute.)

You remember how you finally made contact with your Inner Child, and how you got support for that Child while you learned to love and respect and heal the parts of you that had been damaged in childhood.

You remember the support network that was so important in your life. You remember each of the people who loved you and helped you, and those you loved and helped and supported as well. (Pause 30 seconds.)

You remember the sharing and the learning to negotiate to get the things you needed while giving the important things that other people needed.

You recall the time when you first felt whole and complete and fully able to love yourself and others. It happened long ago. You remember the joy you felt with your new-found strength. (Pause 30 seconds.)

You review the achievements and the wonderful relationships that developed and continued. As you review your life, you think back over the many years since you took new paths and new directions, and recall where these paths and directions have led you.

You think of the people who loved you and supported you unconditionally at all the various stages of your life. You think of the people who challenged you to go further, to try more, to grow, to learn, to love.

You appreciate how different people have been so important to you at different times, in the course of your rich and satisfying life.

As you review, you reflect on the things you have done that you are so proud of, the things that have made a real contribution to life and to living.

Then you reflect on the things you wish you had done differently . . . things you did, using the best resources you had at the time . . . and as you review them, you remember that yes, if you had been older and wiser, with more resources, you would have done things differently. And once more, you acknowledge that each time you did the very best you could. (Pause 30 seconds.)

You love who you were at each stage in your long life. You forgive yourself, and you offer thanks that you've been allowed to take this journey. You offer thanks for the trials that helped you learn and helped you become who you are. You offer thanks for the resources that were provided. (Pause 30 seconds.) As you prepare to release this lifetime, you find yourself anticipating with joy your next step into the unknown.

When you're ready, allow your awareness to gently return to this time and this room. Write about your experiences, including as much as you can remember. If you missed any of the visualization, go back and read it in your Workbook.

When you've completed writing, take a few minutes to complete Worksheet #21.

## Worksheet #21: Your Future

(1) What goals did you visualize achieving later in your life? _____

_____

(2) Are these goals you hope to achieve in your lifetime? _____

_____

(3) What support systems will you need in order to accomplish these goals?

_____

(4) Who are the people you'll need to challenge you? _____

_____

(5) Who will you need to listen to you? _____

_____

(6) Who will you need to help you solve the problems? _____

_____

(7) Who will you need to help you do the work? _____

_____

(8) Who are the people that will affirm you just for being you, no matter

what happens? _____

(9) Are these people in your life now? _____

(10) If not, where are you going to find them? _____

_____

Join your small group and take a few minutes to share the important parts
of this experience.

## Future Nurturing Exchanges

Use this time to make contracts for future Nurturing Exchanges. You have
several options:

(1) You can arrange with one or several other people in this program to
exchange nurturing activities.

(2) You can repeat this program and invite new people to join you.

(3) You can ask for the nurturing you need from people in your existing
support system — without creating a Nurturing Exchange agreement.

(4) You can create an advanced Nurturing Exchange group, using the
guidelines below.

### INSTRUCTIONS FOR ADVANCED NURTURING EXCHANGE GROUPS

The following guidelines for the structure of the advanced Nurturing Exchange groups (an ideal size is six to 12 people) are strongly recommended:

(1) Plan the time and place of your first meeting and choose a leader for
the first session. At each meeting, choose a leader for the following meeting.

(2) Choose one person in the group to communicate any necessary information to all group members between sessions.

(3) Limit this group to those people who have completed the *Parenting
Each Other* program.

(4) Reaffirm the commitments you made when you began the *Parenting Each Other* program.

(5) Choose someone to provide appropriate music to set the tone of each meeting.

(6) Decide whether you prefer to have all participants do the same Nurturing Exchange at each session or to have individually chosen Nurturing Exchanges and have several different activities occurring simultaneously.

(7) If you choose individual activities, each person who wants a particular type of nurturing should be responsible for bringing the appropriate types of materials to the meeting place.

(8) Allow time at the beginning of each meeting to negotiate which Nurturing Exchanges will take place.

(9) Each time the group meets, each person who attends should experience both nurturing and being nurtured.

(10) Shift partners frequently, so that your Inner Child learns that nurturing can come from many sources.

(11) Allow sufficient time for processing the feelings and experiences within each meeting time.

Follow the instructions of the Timekeeper and meet with others who share your interests.

### CLOSING EXERCISE

Take a large sheet of paper. Tape it on your back. Using a crayon or light marking pen, write a positive comment about the person on the papers of as many different people as you can during the next few minutes. When the Timekeeper tells you to stop, take your paper off your back and read it. These are the strokes that other people in the group have for you.

Now in the small group — or in the entire group, if there are no more than 16 participants — stand up and read aloud the strokes you received. After each person is through, applaud and move on to the next.

## Closing Song

We will end the meeting with the song, "I Love Myself" (p. 40).

### SUGGESTED ONGOING ACTIVITIES

Set aside 10 or 15 minutes every day to converse with your Inner Child. Find out how old your Inner Child is, ask what she needs and do what you can to be supportive.

Keep a journal, including the nurturing you want, the nurturing you get, the nurturing you give to other people, and your responses to these experiences.

Read the following books related to Session 14:

*To Take A Dare,* Paul Zindel.
*Jacob Have I Loved,* Katherine Paterson.
*Island Of Blue Dolphins,* Scott O'Dell.
*Grounding Of Group Six,* Julian F. Thomson.
*The Pistachio Prescription* and *There's A Bat In Bunk Five,* Paula Danziger.
*Mom, The Wolfman, And Me,* Norma Klein.

Read any of the following books about healthy growth and healthy relationships:

*Watership Down,* Richard Adams.
*Free To Be You And Me,* Marlo Thomas.
*A Wrinkle In Time; A Swiftly Tilting Planet,* and *A Wind In The Door,* Madeline L'Engle.
*What's Happening To Me?,* Peter Mayle.
*Walt Disney's Uncle Remus Stories,* Transcribed by Joel Chandler Harris.
*Did I Ever Tell You How Lucky You Are?,* Dr. Seuss.
*Are You There, God? It's Me, Margaret, Then Again, Maybe I Won't, Deenie, SuperFudge; Blubber;* and *Forever,* Judy Blume.
*Little House On The Prairie,* series, Laura Ingalls Wilder.
*Chocolate War; I Am The Cheese; The Bumblebee Flies Anyway,* Robert Corimer.

These are useful recovery books for children — real or Inner:

*Some Secrets Are For Sharing,* Randy Winston Hillier.
*What's "Drunk," Mama?,* Al-Anon Family Group Headquarters, Inc.
*An Elephant In The Living Room,* Jill Hastings and Marion Typp.
*My Dad Loves Me, My Dad Has a Disease,* Claudia Black.
*Welcome Home,* J. A. Jance.

Keep a stack of your favorite children's books and read them periodically, either to yourself, to children or have them read to you.

Read any parts of *Recovery From Co-dependency: It's Never Too Late To Reclaim Your Childhood* that you haven't yet completed or review any parts of special interest to you.

Read *Becoming the Way We Are* by Pam Levin

Read *Growing Up Again* by Jean Clarke and Connie Dawson.

Read *Homecoming* by John Bradshaw.

Provide some sort of treat for your Inner Child every day. It could be a single flower, an ice cream cone, time listening to your favorite music, a nap, a package of marbles or jacks, or quiet time for yourself.

Be gentle to yourself and others. Get a massage at least once a week. Fly a kite. Splash in a mud puddle. Roll down a grassy hill.

Have a good life.

APPENDIX

# How To Organize
# This Program

Instructions For The Organizer(s) ................................................. 151

Program Announcement .............................................................. 154

Timekeeper's Guides For Introductory Sessions

    1: Thinking About Parenting Each Other ................................... 155

    2: Creating A Safe Environment For Parenting Each Other ............ 161

Timekeeper's Guides For Parenting Sessions
General Guidelines For Sessions 3-14 ............................................ 165

    3: Creating Boundaries ........................................................ 167

    4: I Don't Know What I Want .................................................. 173

    5: Learning To Ask .............................................................. 177

    6: Holding And Touching ...................................................... 181

7: Asking For Closeness .............................................. 185

8: Why? Why? Why? .................................................. 189

9: Just How Powerful Am I? ........................................ 193

10: Making Mistakes Is Okay ...................................... 197

11: Negotiation Skills .............................................. 201

12: More About Boundaries ........................................ 205

13: Parenting Your Own Inner Child .............................. 209

14: Leaving Home .................................................. 213

References ............................................................ 217

Bibliography (Children's Books) .................................... 219

# INSTRUCTIONS
## For The Organizer(s)

The *Parenting Each Other* program may be organized and carried out by any individual or committee of several individuals willing to take responsibility for creating the necessary structure for the program. No special training is required.

*Parenting Each Other* is not a psychotherapy program nor is it a substitute for therapy, but it may bring to the surface issues that are best dealt with in therapy. If the organizer is not a mental health professional, it is important to arrange for backup assistance and consultation from a qualified psychotherapist, in case a participant gets in touch with issues the program is not designed to handle. If the participant does not already have a therapist, the consultant can make referral suggestions and/or provide direct assistance.

This program is designed for use by support groups of varying size. The recommended minimum group size is six participants. There are no maximum limits as long as the physical space is large enough to accommodate the entire group.

In each session, all participants will meet together, and a designated Timekeeper will follow the instructions in the Timekeeper's Guides and lead participants through a series of exercises.

The Timekeeper may be any participant in the program or a professional who will lead the group through the entire program. Leaderless support groups should rotate the Timekeeper role or have a small committee responsible for managing the structure of each meeting.

The organizer will act as Timekeeper for the first two sessions. In addition, before the first session, the organizer(s) need to:

151

- Arrange for a meeting time and space. An ideal space would be a private, carpeted room, large enough to accommodate your participants when seated in groups of six chairs arranged in circles. (Provisions for privacy should be made. Some of the activities will be loud, and others would look strange to somebody passing by and looking through a window. If there are large windows that people can see through, they will need to be covered during some of the exercises.)
- Invite people to attend the program — see sample program announcement in Appendix, page 154.
- Arrange for a tape player or sound system powerful enough to enable members of the group to easily hear the words and music of the tapes you will play.
- At *each* session you will need a tape of "The Greatest Love of All," from the Arista album, "Whitney Houston," by Whitney Houston, or from the Warner Brothers album, "Weekend in L.A.," by George Benson (words and music by Linda Creed and Michael Masser). You will also need a tape of "I Love Myself," by Jai Josefs (from the album "Loving Yourself," available from Hay House, Inc., P.O. Box 2212, Santa Monica, CA 90406, 213-394-7445) for Sessions 3 to 14.
- You will need at least one or two of the following tapes or compositions to provide background music during exercises:
  "Golden Voyage," by Georgia Kelley
  "Starborn Suite," "Spectrum Suite" or "Comfort Zone," all by Stephen Halpern
  "Deep Breakfast," by Ray Lynch (highly recommended for the two-year-old exercises in Session 3)
  "The Quiet," by John Michael Talbott
  "Fairy Ring," by Michael Rowland
  "Piano Means Soft," by Charlie Thweat
  "Ambience," by Paul Winter
  "Gone like the Sand and the Foam," by Dan Fogelberg
  "Brandenburg Concertos," by J.S. Bach
  "Canon in G" by J. Pachelbel
  Other Baroque music
- Have copies of necessary handouts available for Sessions 1 and 2.
- Have a timer available that will ring or buzz at the end of a designated period. A wristwatch timer or a kitchen timer is suitable.
- Have tapes of the visualizations in Sessions 3 to 14 available for those sessions. You can make your own recording of the visualizations or you can purchase the tapes from Empowerment Systems, (2275 E. Arapahoe Rd., Ste. 306, Littleton, Colorado 80122, 303-794-5379.)

- Have large sheets of newsprint and markers available during Sessions 1, 2 and 14.
- Provide nametags for participants. If the group size is 12 or fewer, the use of nametags can be discontinued after the first three sessions.
- Calculate the expenses for the program and decide how they will be shared. The organizer may charge a fee to cover expenses or ask for contributions at each session. If the organizer is a professional who will be leading the entire program, a charge for professional time is appropriate.
- Arrange to collect any money necessary to support the program during each session, if necessary.
- Before Sessions 1 and 2, write the Worksheet questions on newsprint, to be posted as they are needed.
- After Session 2, when participants have committed to the program, prepare a master list of all participants. The list should include first name, last initial and telephone number.
- Arrange with a local bookstore to have copies of the following books available for purchase:
    *Recovery From Co-Dependency: It's Never Too Late To Reclaim Your Childhood,* by Laurie Weiss and Jonathan B. Weiss
    *Becoming the Way We Are,* by Pam Levin
    *Self-Esteem: A Family Affair,* by Jean Illsley Clarke
    *Growing Up Again,* by Jean Illsley Clarke and Connie Dawson
    *Parent Effectiveness Training,* by Thomas Gordon
    *Homecoming,* by John Bradshaw
- Recruit Timekeepers for the succeeding sessions. If the group size is over 30 people, designate an assistant Timekeeper for each session. The responsibilities of the Timekeeper will be:
1. To make certain that the physical space is set up;
2. To make certain that the materials necessary for the session are readily available;
3. To read the instructions for each exercise aloud and guide discussion if necessary;
4. To protect the privacy of the group by answering the doorbell, opening or closing windows and dealing with interruptions;
5. To act as Timekeeper, following the instructions in the Timekeeper's Guide and modifying them whenever change seems to be appropriate;
6. To play the designated music during different segments of each session;
7. To recruit the next designated Timekeeper: Choose Timekeepers for Sessions 3 and 4 during Session 2. After Session 2, choose the Timekeeper so that he or she will have two weeks to prepare for the session.

# *Program Announcement*

## ARE YOU READY FOR A NEW EXPERIENCE IN RECOVERY?

Learn to nurture your Inner Child, in a new *Parenting Each Other* support program (PEO). A new support group is starting, using *An Action Plan For Your Inner Child: Parenting Each Other.*

For more information, call:                    Beginning Date _____

_____          Day _____

                                             Time _____

                                             Location _____

## SUPPORT PROGRAM OVERVIEW

• PEO (Parenting Each Other) is a structured program for grown-ups who missed important nurturing experiences in childhood.

• PEO is divided into 14 three-hour sessions. Each session contains structured experiences and writing and discussion about those experiences.

• The first two introductory meetings are open to anyone who is interested.

• The 12 Parenting Sessions are open only to those who commit to honor a set of agreements designed to create safety, trust and consistency for all participants. After the first Parenting Session, no new participants may join the program.

• PEO is a program where your Inner Child can experience healthy parenting in a safe environment.

• PEO is a place to learn the skills you need to become a healthy parent for your Inner Child and for your own children.

*Timekeeper's Guide For*
*Introductory Sessions*

## SESSION 1
## INTRODUCTORY MEETING

# THINKING ABOUT
# PARENTING EACH OTHER

Before the meeting, gather the necessary materials:

- Nametags
- Two tapes of background music
- One tape of "The Greatest Love of All"
- Sheets of newsprint with the items for each worksheet, the instructions for each exercise and the optional activities to do between sessions, all printed in large lettering
- Two copies of *An Action Plan For Your Inner Child: Parenting Each Other*
- A timer
- A tape player (be sure you know how to use it)
- Masking tape to hang the newsprint
- Handouts: The Self-Assessment Questionnaire on pages 12-13, the lyrics to "The Greatest Love of All" on page 15
- Writing paper

Arrange the chairs in circles of six facing each other.

Before the session starts, ask several participants if they are willing to read sections of the text aloud. Call on only those participants to read.

155

Know where participants can purchase *An Action Plan For Your Inner Child: Parenting Each Other.*

Reward promptness by beginning the meeting on time.

Introduce the meeting by reading the following:

*Welcome to the first session of Parenting Each Other. My name is _____ _____, and I'm serving as the Timekeeper for this session. Parenting Each Other is a program for adults who have difficulty nurturing themselves, because they missed important nurturing experiences when they were children. Many of us sometimes experience feeling like a child in a grown-up body, wishing for someone to care for us and teach us how to manage our world. This Inner Child is a part of each of us. This vulnerable, valuable part of us still needs the nurturing we missed when we were children. We all still need some parenting.*

*Some of us may identify ourselves as Adult Children of Alcoholics, as Adult Children of Dysfunctional Families, as addicts or as co-dependents. This program refers to us all as "Adult Children." In this program, we will learn to give and receive the nurturing needed by the lonely, unhappy Inner Child. This session, Thinking About Parenting Each Other, introduces this program.*

*People learn to nurture themselves by being nurtured. Adult Children who missed out on many of the ordinary and important nurturing experiences of childhood often are unsuccessful at self-nurturing. Although we can often learn to parent others successfully by reading and studying, we have great difficulty parenting ourselves. Instead, we continue to criticize ourselves unmercifully. This program provides those necessary nurturing exchanges the Adult Child needs to learn to successfully nurture him- or herself.*

*Children of different ages need very different types of parenting. This program uses guided imagery, writing, group discussion, sharing, music and practical instruction to create a safe and supportive space for the Inner Child to receive this parenting. Participants engage in specific nurturing exchanges with each other to nurture the Inner Child through the important stages of development.*

*This program consists of 14 three-hour sessions. We will meet each _____ (day of the week) from _____ (time) to _____ (time). We will start each session promptly at _____ (time).*

*The first two sessions remain open. Anyone interested in participating is welcome to attend. After the third session, the meetings will be closed to newcomers, so that there will be a common level of information among participants and to make it easier to feel safe with people we already know.*

*The program uses a variety of worksheets and exercises that we will do together during each session.*

*Please give your undivided attention to others when they are sharing. Do not interrupt or attempt to "fix" another person. If you choose not to share, say "I pass" when it is your turn. Keep confidential anything you learn about others.*

*Optional activities to do between sessions are suggested, to enhance your learning and integration of the material.*

*All participants will need to purchase a personal copy of the* Parenting Each Other *workbook before the third session. You can purchase your copy at* _____

(name of bookstore).

(If applicable: *This program is self-supporting through our own contributions. Our expenses are approximately $*_____ *for each meeting. Please make your contribution at this time to avoid interrupting the meeting.* Pass an envelope, jar or basket.)

*Throughout the session, individuals who have agreed to do so will be asked to read aloud the portions of the workbook that introduce each exercise. If you would like to be one of the readers, please tell me during a break.*

*In Session 1, Thinking About Parenting Each Other, the author describes an experience of receiving healthy parenting during a stressful time in her life.*

Ask the first reader: _____, *will you please read the section entitled What Is Healthy Parenting, on pages 1 and 2.*

After the section is read, thank the reader and hang up the newsprint with the questions for the Worksheet before you instruct people to complete the Worksheet. Give the following instructions:

*Take 10 minutes to complete Worksheet #1. If you have workbooks, you can complete the Worksheet in your workbook. If not, you can use scratch paper to write out the answers.*

Play a music tape from the list, softly in the background, as people fill out each Worksheet and as they share with each other. Turn the tape off when individuals are reading the introduction to each exercise.

At eight minutes, announce: *You have two minutes left to complete the Worksheet.* At 10 minutes, make this announcement:

*Please stop now. You have 10 minutes to share what you have written with other members of your small group. Have the first person share one item, then go on to the second person, then the third, until each person in the group has had an opportunity to share one item. If you have time, you can repeat the procedure with the next item. Don't worry if you don't have a chance to share everything on your Worksheet.*

*Please allow approximately equal time for each group member. Give your undivided attention to others when they are sharing. Do not interrupt or attempt to "fix" another person. If you choose not to share, say "I pass" when it is your turn. Keep confidential anything you learn about others.*

At five minutes, announce: *Half the time is up.* At eight minutes, announce: *You have two minutes left.* At 10 minutes, announce: *Please stop now.*

Stop music. Post Worksheet #2. Ask the next reader: _____, *will you please read the section Adult Children Need Parenting, on page 3?*

After the section is read, thank the reader and give these instructions:

*You have five minutes to complete Worksheet #2. I'll warn you shortly before your time is up.*

Start music. At three minutes, announce: *You have two minutes left.* At five minutes, announce: *Please stop now.*

*Share what you have written with your group. Each person should have the opportunity to share the answers to question one, then each person should share the answers to question two. Next, each person can share information about the response to one authority figure in your current life. Finally, share what you have learned by answering these questions. You have 15 minutes.*

At eight minutes, announce: *You have seven minutes left.* At 15 minutes, announce: *Please stop now.*

Stop music. Post Worksheet #3. Ask the next reader: _____, *will you please read the section I Can Do It Myself, on page 5?*

After the section is read, thank the reader and give these instructions:

*You have five minutes to complete Worksheet #3. I'll warn you shortly before your time is up.*

Start music. At three minutes, announce: *You have two minutes left.* At five minutes, make this announcement:

*Please stop now. You have 10 minutes to share your answers to Worksheet #3 in your group. Let each group member share responses to question one before moving on to question two, etc. I'll warn you when half the time is up and two minutes before it's time to stop.*

At five minutes, announce: *You have five minutes left.* At eight minutes, announce: *You have two minutes left.* At 10 minutes, announce: *Please stop now.*

Stop music. Post Worksheet #4. Ask the next reader: _____, *will you please read the section Why Parent Each Other, on page 6?*

After the section is read, thank the reader and give the following instructions:

*You have seven minutes to complete Worksheet #4. I'll warn you shortly before your time is up.*

Start music.

At five minutes, announce: *Two-minute warning.* At seven minutes, an-nounce: *Please stop now. You will have 10 minutes to share your answers about one person you parent with the other members of your group.*

At five minutes, announce: *Half the time is up.* At eight minutes, announce: *Two-minute warning.* At 10 minutes, announce: *Please stop now.*

Stop music. Post Worksheet #5. Ask the next reader: _____, *will you please read Parenting Without Exploitation, on pages 7 and 8.*

After the section is read, thank the reader and give the following instruc-tions:

*You have three minutes to complete Worksheet #5. I'll warn you shortly before your time is up.*

Start music.

Announce: *One-and-a-half minutes.* At three minutes, announce: *Please stop now. You have 15 minutes to share your responses and your reasons for your responses. Each person share responses to question one before moving on to question two, etc.*

Every two-and-a-half minutes, announce: *You should be moving on to question two (three, four, etc.)* Announce when 15 minutes is up.

Stop music. Read aloud the section Nurturing Exchange. Post Work-sheet #6. Give these instructions:

*Use about five minutes to complete Worksheet #6.* At three minutes, announce: *Two-minute warning.*

At five minutes, announce: *Please stop now. Take 10 minutes to share your responses to Worksheet #6 with your group. First each of you share your response to question one, then to question two, etc.*

Start music. At five minutes, announce: *Half the time is up.* At eight min-utes: *You have two minutes left.* At 10 minutes: *Please stop now.*

Stop music. Read the introduction to the exercise Accepting Compliments (p. 10), then the instructions for the exercise (pp. 10-11). Post the instructions on newsprint. Give these instructions:

*Now choose a partner. You have three minutes to tell your partner the compliment, practice turning it down, then accepting it and then embellish-ing it. Begin now.*

Start music. Give a warning one minute before the time is up. At three minutes, announce: *Please stop. Now switch roles with your partner and repeat the exercise, so your partner has the opportunity to practice accepting a compliment that has been turned down before.*

Give a one-minute warning. At three minutes, announce: *Please stop now. Take about three minutes each to share how you felt during each phase of giving and receiving your compliments.*

Allow six minutes. Give a three-minute warning. Announce when the time is up. Stop music. Ask the next reader:

_____, *will you read aloud the section entitled What To Expect from Parenting Each Other, on page 11?*

Thank the reader. Post a list of activities to do between sessions. Announce: *These are optional activities to do between sessions, to enhance your learning and integration of the material.*

Read the activities. Read aloud the preparation for the next session. Pass out copies of the Self-Assessment Questionnaire and remind the participants:

*Remember, you can purchase your copy of* An Action Plan For Your Inner Child: Parenting Each Other *at* _____
(name of bookstore).
*If you or a friend has a copy, we recommend that you read the first part of Chapter Two before the next session.*

Pass out copies of the words to "The Greatest Love of All."

*We will finish with a closing song. Please help put the room back in order before you leave. Now, form a large circle, join hands and sing together the unofficial theme song of the Adult Children's movement, "The Greatest Love of All."* Play the song on the tape player and sing along. When the song is over, announce:

*Thank you for coming. Our next meeting will be at* _____
(place), *at* _____ (time and day). *See you next time.*

*Timekeeper's*
*Guide For*

SESSION 2
INTRODUCTORY MEETING

# CREATING A SAFE ENVIRONMENT FOR PARENTING EACH OTHER

Before the meeting, gather these materials:

- Nametags
- Two tapes of background music
- One tape of "The Greatest Love of All"
- Sheets of newsprint, with the items for each Worksheet, the situations for discussion of Agreement #2 and the optional activities to do between sessions, all printed in large lettering
- Two copies of *An Action Plan For Your Inner Child: Parenting Each Other*
- A timer
- A tape player
- Masking tape or some other means of hanging the newsprint
- Handouts: Copies of the Self-Assessment Questionnaire (pages 12-13), lyrics to "The Greatest Love of All." (page 15), copies of Commitments (p. 23), copies of Agreements to Create Safety, Trust and Consistency (pp. 28-29), one index card for each participant

Arrange the chairs in circles of six. Before the session starts, ask several participants to volunteer to read aloud. Reward promptness by beginning the meeting on time.

161

Introduce the meeting by reading the following:

*Welcome to the second session of* Parenting Each Other. *My name is ____,*
*_____ and I'm the Timekeeper for this session.*
*This program helps Adult Children learn to give and receive the nurturing*
*needed by the lonely, unhappy Inner Child.*

*People learn to nurture themselves by being nurtured. Adult Children who*
*missed out on many of the ordinary and important nurturing experiences*
*of childhood often are unsuccessful at self-nurturing. Although we can*
*often learn to parent others successfully by reading and studying, we have*
*great difficulty parenting ourselves. Instead, we criticize ourselves unmerci-*
*fully. This program provides those necessary nurturing exchanges the Adult*
*Child needs to learn to successfully nurture him- or herself.*

Post Worksheet #7. Ask the first reader:

*_____, will you please read the first paragraph in Session 2?*

Then give these instructions:

*You have five minutes to complete Worksheet #7. I'll warn you shortly*
*before your time is up.*

Start music. At three minutes, announce: *You have two minutes left to*
*complete the Worksheet.* At five minutes, announce: *Please stop now. In your*
*group take 10 minutes to share your responses to the Worksheet. First have*
*each member share your Inner Child statements. Then share the Inner*
*Parent statements, then the Adult statements.*

At eight minutes, announce: *Two-minute warning.* At 10 minutes: *Please*
*stop now.*

Stop music. Post Worksheet #8. Ask the next reader:

*_____, will you please read the section The Power Of Survival*
*Decisions, on page 18?*

After the section is read, thank the first reader and ask the next reader:

*_____, will you please read the section entitled Problems With*
*Survival Decisions, on page 19?*

After the section is read, thank the reader and give the following instructions:

*Take 10 minutes to complete Worksheet #8.*

Start music. At five minutes: *You have five minutes left.* At 10 minutes:
*Please stop now. In your group, share your responses to the questions. This will*
*be a quick sharing. Let each person share two or three answers to question*
*one before the whole group proceeds to question two. Let each person share*
*two or three answers to question two before proceeding to question three. You*
*have 20 minutes for this exercise.*

At the end of 10 minutes, remind the group that they should be moving on
to question four. At 18 minutes, give a two-minute warning. At 20 minutes
announce: *Please stop now.* Stop music.

*The next 12 meetings are Parenting Each Other Sessions.* Ask the next reader: _____, *please read the beginning of the description of the Parenting Sessions on page 21.*

Allow the participant to read approximately half of the section, thank him/ her and ask the next reader to continue to the end of the section. Thank the reader, pass out the statements of commitment and say:

*I will now pass out the commitment statements from page 23 in your Workbook. This is a challenging program; making an informed commitment to participate will help you stay focused on achieving your goals. Each of the following Parenting Each Other sessions will have a similar structure. Read each paragraph aloud in your small group and allow each person to briefly share their immediate response to that paragraph. When you are through, if you are ready to make a commitment to the program, sign and date your commitment statement. You have 25 minutes.*

Start music. Announce the time after 10 minutes and after 20 minutes. When 25 minutes are up, announce: *Please stop now.* Stop music. Announce:

*If you wish to participate in the remainder of the program, you need to make the following agreements to create safety, trust and consistency in our environment.*

Ask the next reader: _____, *will you please read the introductory paragraph about these agreements on pages 23 and 24?*

After the section is read, thank the reader, hand out copies of the agreements and give these instructions:

*I'm passing out a short copy of the agreements to each of you. We will read explanations of each agreement and you will have an opportunity to discuss them in your group, to be sure you understand what you are agreeing to do. After you've completed a discussion of each agreement and agreed to honor it, initial it.*

Ask the next reader:

_____, *please read Agreement #1 (page 24).* Thank the reader and say:

*Each person in the group now has the opportunity to briefly state your understanding of what this agreement means. You'll have five minutes to do so. When you're through and are ready to initial the agreement, please do so.*

Start music. Time the group for five minutes. Stop music. Ask the next reader:

_____, *please read Agreement #2, on page 24.*

Then say:

*To clarify your understanding of this agreement, discuss with your small group some possible responses to the following situations:*

Post these situations and read them:

1. Someone talks about his or her father promising to come to a school program and not showing up.

2. Someone gives you advice you don't want.

3. Someone talks about feeling shamed by what they have revealed to you in the group.

Give these instructions:

*Spend five minutes discussing possible responses to these situations. Spend an additional five minutes discussing any part of the agreement that was stated. If you have a workbook you can find the full discussion on page 24.*

Start music. Inform the group when the first five minutes is up and when 10 minutes is up. Stop music.

Repeat the procedure used for reading and discussing Agreement #1 for the rest of the agreements. When all of the agreements have been completed, ask the next reader:

_____, *will you please read the section entitled Continuing This Program on page 29?*

Thank the reader. Then pass out the index cards and say:

*Please sign and date your list of agreements if you wish to continue in this program. Please fill out an index card with your name, address and phone number, indicating that you intend to continue the program. At the bottom write the statement, "I have signed my commitment sheet and my participant agreements." Please leave your index cards with me, so that we can compile a list of people participating in the program.*

*For the next session, bring your workbook, the Self-Assessment Question-naire, a pair of shoes with laces, socks and a sweater or jacket. You may wear these to the session.*

If the leadership is to be rotated, announce:

*We need volunteers to act as Timekeepers for the next two sessions. If you are willing to act as Timekeeper, please see me after this meeting. Activities to do between sessions are on the posted list.*

Pass out copies of the words to "The Greatest Love of All."

*We will finish with a closing song. Please help put the room back in order before you leave. Now, form a circle, join hands and sing together the unofficial theme song of the Adult Children's movement,* "The Greatest Love of All."

Play the song on the tape player and sing along. When the song is over, say:

*Thank you for coming. Our next meeting will be at* _____ (place), *at* _____ (time and day). *See you next time.*

*Timekeeper's Guide For*
*Parenting Sessions*

# GENERAL GUIDELINES
# FOR SESSIONS 3 to 14

1. At least a week before the meeting, read through the session and the specific instructions for the meeting you are going to lead.

2. Make certain that you have a taped copy of the evening's visualization exercise, or that you have rehearsed the visualization and are prepared to read it during the session. You can make your own tape, if you like, so that you can be a participant as well as a Timekeeper.

3. Be certain you know how to operate the tape player and timer before the meeting. Have your music tapes prepared and cued before the meeting begins.

4. Arrive early and be sure the room is set up properly.

5. Before the meeting starts, ask several participants if they are willing to read sections of the text aloud. Be sure there are enough volunteers to read all of the necessary sections. Call on only those participants to read.

6. Keep careful track of the time and be firm about moving people on to the next exercise in a timely way.

7. You may participate in a timed exercise, as long as you set the timer and make the appropriate announcements.

8. Ask a group member to phone each person who is absent, in order to support their attendance at the next meeting.

9. Be sure the room is back in order at the end of the session you are leading.

10. Be sure the timekeeper is chosen.

11. Share the information you have about how to use the equipment and tapes with the next timekeeper.

12. The background music should be turned on every time there is a written or sharing exercise. It should be turned off when someone is reading aloud.

*Timekeeper's*
*Guide For*

SESSION 3

# CREATING
# BOUNDARIES

Be sure you have reviewed the information in General Guidelines for the Timekeeper: Sessions 3-14.

Before the meeting, be sure you have the necessary materials:

- Nametags
- Two tapes of background music
- One tape of "The Greatest Love of All"
- One tape of "I Love Myself"
- One copy of *An Action Plan For Your Inner Child: Parenting Each Other*
- A timer
- A tape player (be sure you know how to use it)

Arrange the chairs in circles of six facing each other.

Reward promptness by beginning the meeting on time.

*Welcome to the third session of* Parenting Each Other. *This is our first Parenting Session, Creating Boundaries. My name is* _____, *and I'm your Timekeeper for this session.*

Ask the first reader: _____, *will you please read the commitment statements, on page 23?*

167

After the section is read, thank the reader and ask the next reader: _____
_____, *will you please read the Agreements to Create Safety, Trust, and Consistency, on pages 28-29?*

After the section is read, thank the reader and give the following instructions:

*We will start this session, as well as the remaining sessions of the program, with a brief time for sharing. During this time you may share anything at all with other members of your small group. You can share experiences from the past week or anything that is important to you at the moment, such as the heavy traffic on the way to the session. You can share important things that you learned between the last session and this one, or activities that you participated in. Remember that there are six people in your group and only 10 minutes for sharing, so please be concise.*

*The first person to share will be the person closest to me; start by saying, "What I feel like saying is . . ." and complete a sentence or two about anything important to you right now. When you are finished, turn to the person on your right and say, ". . . and that's what I feel like saying. What do you feel like saying, (Jim, Mary, etc.)?" The next person then says, "What I feel like saying is . . ." Keep going around the group until I tell you it's time to stop. If you have nothing to share, say, "I pass."*

*You will have 10 minutes to share. I will give you a warning two minutes before the time is complete. Start now.*

Begin the music faintly in the background. Announce the two-minute warning after eight minutes and say, *Please stop now,* at the end of 10 minutes. Stop music.

Read the introduction to Session 3, starting with "Your two-year-old . . ." on page 31. When you have finished reading that first paragraph, give these instructions:

*Please take out the Self-Assessment Questionnaires you filled out at Session 1. Use the next three minutes to read your workbook section entitled Self-Assessment Questionnaire, on page 31.*

Start music. Time for three minutes. Announce when time is up.

Stop music. Ask the next reader:

_____, *will you please read the introduction to our next exercise Boundaries, on pages 31-32?*

After the section is read, thank the reader and give the following instructions:

*Please turn to Worksheet #9: Procrastination, on page 32. You have five minutes to complete Item Number one on the worksheet.*

Start music. At three minutes, announce a two-minute warning, and say *Please stop,* at five minutes.

Stop music. Ask the next reader: _____, *will you*

After the section is read, thank the reader and give the following instructions:

*You will have three minutes to share your modified answers to Question one. Please move quickly. I will not give you a two minute warning, but will inform you when the three minutes are up. If you run out of time before you run out of items to share, let the other items go.*

Start music. When three minutes have passed, say, *Please stop.* Give the following instructions:

*Now take five minutes to quickly jot down your answers to Questions 2, 3, 4 and 5 on your Worksheet.*

When five minutes have passed, say, *Please stop.* Give the following instructions:

*You will have another five minutes to briefly share the answers to Questions 2, 3 and 4. Choose one item from Question 5 and share that as well. I will tell you when the time is up.*

When five minutes have passed, say, *Please stop.* Give the following instructions:

*Now take two minutes to complete number six on your Worksheet. Begin.*

When two minutes have passed, say *Please stop.*

Stop music. Give the following instructions:

*Now share again. For each item on your list, say either, "I'm eventually going to do . . . (whatever it is)" or "I'm not willing to do . . . (whatever it is)." You may choose to share any commitments you make to complete items by a particular time. You will have five minutes for this sharing. Remember to be responsive to each other. Begin now.*

Start music. When five minutes have passed, say *Please stop.*

Have all participants take a 10-minute break. At 10 minutes, stop music and ask participants to form a large circle.

Read the introduction to the Centering Ritual. Play the tape of "The Greatest Love of All" loudly. Stop the tape promptly when the song is over. Ask participants to return to their small group areas. When people are settled, read the following instructions:

*Now prepare to experience what it's like to have the normal behaviors of a two-year-old child responded to appropriately with love, support and appropriate limits. Sit quietly with nothing in your lap and follow along with the visualization.*

Play the tape recording of the visualization or, if you are reading it, play quiet music in the background as you read. Read Slowly! When you have finished the visualization, give these instructions:

*Take five minutes to write about your experience.* Start music. After five minutes say, *Please stop now.*

*You will have 30 minutes to discuss the answers to the questions on page 36. I will tell you when 15 minutes and 25 minutes have passed and when to stop.*

Start music. Announce times at 15 minutes and 25 minutes. At 30 minutes, stop the discussion and make the following announcement:

*Take a five-minute break. Then return to your group and read the instructions for the Nurturing Exchange on page 36. We will start small group discussion of these instructions in 12 minutes.*

After 12 minutes have passed, announce: *Discuss and clarify the instructions and any reservations you may have in your small group. You will have five minutes for this discussion. If you need more time, please inform the Timekeeper.*

(Timekeeper: You have the option of giving the groups an additional five minutes.) Announce when time is up. Give the following instructions:

*Now choose a partner. Decide which role you will take and proceed with the exchange. I'll give a two-minute warning to inform the parenters of the two-year-olds that it's time to grow up. I'll tell you when to stop. Begin now.*

At eight minutes announce the two-minute warning. At nine minutes announce: *Parenters, tell your two-year-olds, "It's time to grow up."* At 10 minutes announce:

*Please stop now. Find your workbook and write about your experience for two or three minutes. When you've finished, share your experience with your partner. In seven minutes we will choose new partners and repeat the exercise. Begin writing now.*

At three minutes, announce: *Please share with your partner now.* At seven minutes, announce:

*Please stop. Now choose a new partner who had the opposite role from yours. You will change roles. Reread the instructions for your new role. We will start the new Nurturing Exchange in five minutes.*

At five minutes say, *Please begin the Nurturing Exchange. I will tell you when the time is up, as I did before.* Give the two-minute warning at eight minutes. At nine minutes, announce: *Parenters, it's time to tell your two-year-olds to grow up.*

At 10 minutes say: *Please stop now. Find your workbook. Write briefly about your experience and share your experience with your partner. You will have seven minutes to write and share.*

At three minutes announce: *Please begin to share with your partner now.* At five minutes announce: *You have two minutes left.* At seven minutes, announce: *Please stop now.*

*Please get phone numbers from at least two people before you leave the session this evening, so that, if you wish to discuss the program between sessions, you'll have somebody to talk to.*

*Between this session and the next, review the list of optional activities. Do as many of them as you want to.*

Stop music. Ask the next reader:

_____, *will you please read aloud Preparation for the Next Session, on page 39?*

After the section is read, thank the reader and give the following instructions:

*We will finish with a new closing song, "I Love Myself," by Jai Josefs. The words are on page 40 of your workbook. Please help put the room back in order before you leave. Now, form a circle, join hands and sing together.*

Play the song on the tape player and sing along. When the song is over, announce:

*Thank you for coming. Our next meeting will be at* _____ (place), *at* _____ (time and day). *See you next time.*

*Timekeeper's*
*Guide For*

# I DON'T KNOW WHAT I WANT

Be sure you have reviewed the information in General Guidelines for the Timekeeper: Sessions 3-14.

Before the meeting, be sure you have the necessary materials:

- Nametags
- Two tapes of background music
- One tape of "The Greatest Love of All"
- One tape of "I Love Myself"
- A timer
- A tapeplayer (be sure you know how to use it)

Arrange the chairs in circles of six facing each other.

Reward promptness by beginning the meeting on time.

*Welcome to the fourth session of Parenting Each Other. My name is* _____, *and I'm your Timekeeper for this session, I Don't Know What I Want.*

Ask the first reader: _____, *will you please read the commitment statements on page 23.*

After the section is read, thank the reader and ask the next reader: _____
_____ *will you please read the Agreements*
*to Create Safety, Trust And Consistency on pages 28-29?*

After the section is read, thank the reader and give the following instructions:

*We will start this session with a brief time for sharing. During this time you may share anything at all with other members of your small group. Remember that there are six people in your small group and only 10 minutes for sharing, so please be concise.*

*The first person to share will be the person closest to me. You will start by saying, "What I feel like saying is . . ." and complete a sentence or two about anything important to you right now. When you are finished, turn to the person on your right and say, ". . . and that's what I feel like saying. What do you feel like saying, (Jim, Mary, etc.)?" The next person then says, "What I feel like saying is . . ." Keep going around the group until it's time to stop. If you have nothing to share, say "I pass."*

*You will have 10 minutes to share. I will give you a warning two minutes before the time is complete. Start now.*

Begin music faintly in the background. Announce the two-minute warning after eight minutes, and say *Please stop now,* at the end of 10 minutes.

Stop music. Read the introduction to I Don't Know What I Want on page 41. Then give the following instructions:

*Please take out the Self-Assessment Questionnaires you filled out at Session 1. Use the next three minutes to review your workbook section entitled Self-Assessment Questionnaire on page 41.*

Start music. Time for three minutes. Announce when time is up. Give the following instructions:

*You have 12 minutes to complete Worksheet #10: Making Choices, on pages 41-43. I will warn you when two minutes remain.*

Announce when six minutes have passed. When 10 minutes have passed, say, *Two-minute warning.* When 12 minutes have passed say, *Please stop now.*

*Now share your answers in your small group. Each person share the answer to the first question before you all move on to the second question. That way everyone will have the opportunity to share, even if you don't get through all the questions.*

*As people share, be sure to acknowledge them by giving them your full attention and thanking them for their input. You will have 15 minutes for sharing. I will inform you when half the time has passed, warn you when only two minutes are remaining and tell you when to stop.*

Tell the group when seven minutes have passed. At 13 minutes say, *Two minute warning.* At 15 minutes say, *Please stop now.*

Have all participants take a 10-minute break. At 10 minutes, stop the music and ask participants to form a large circle.

Read the introduction to the Centering Ritual on page 43. Play the tape of "The Greatest Love of All" loudly. Stop the tape promptly when the song is over. Ask participants to return to their small group areas. When people are settled, read the following instructions:

*Now prepare to experience what it's like to have the normal behaviors of a one-year-old child responded to appropriately with love, support and appropriate limits. Sit quietly with nothing in your lap and follow along with the visualization.*

Play the tape of the visualization or, if you are reading it, play quiet music in the background as you read. Read Slowly! When you have finished the visualization, give the following instructions:

*Take five minutes to write about your experience.*

Start music. After five minutes say, *Please stop now.*

*You willl have 30 minutes to discuss, in your small group, the answers to the questions on pages 45-46. I will tell you when 15 minutes and 25 minutes have passed, and when to stop.*

Announce times at 15 minutes and 25 minutes. At 30 minutes, stop the discussion and make the following announcement:

*Take a five-minute break. Then return to your small group and read the instructions for the Nurturing Exchange, on pages 46-47. We will start small group discussion of these instructions in 12 minutes.*

After 12 minutes have passed, announce: *Discuss and clarify the instructions and any reservations you may have in your small group. You will have five minutes for this discussion. If you need more time, please inform the Timekeeper.*

(Timekeeper: You have the option of giving the groups an additional five minutes at this point.) Announce when time is up. Give the following instructions:

*Now, choose a partner. Decide which role you will take and proceed with the exchange. I'll give a two minute warning to inform the parenters of the one-year-olds that it's time to grow up. I'll tell you when to stop. Begin now.*

At eight minutes, announce the two-minute warning. At nine minutes, announce: *Parenters, tell your one-year-olds, "It's time to grow up."* At 10 minutes announce:

*Please stop. Find your workbook and write about your experience for two or three minutes. When you've finished your writing, share your experience with your partner. In seven minutes we will choose new partners and repeat the exercise. Begin writing now.*

At three minutes, announce: *Please share with your partner now.* At seven minutes, announce:

*Please stop. Now, choose a new partner who had the opposite role from yours. You will change roles. Review the instructions for your new role. We will start the new Nurturing Exchange in five minutes.*

At five minutes say, *Please begin the Nurturing Exchange. I will tell you when the time is up, as I did before.* Give the two-minute warning at eight minutes. At nine minutes, announce: *Parenters, it's time to tell your one-year-olds to grow up.*

At 10 minutes say, *Please stop now. Find your workbook. Write briefly about your experience and share your experience with your partner. You have seven minutes to write and share.*

At three minutes announce: *Please begin to share with your partner now.* At five minutes, announce: *You have two minutes left.* At seven minutes, announce: *Please stop now.*

Stop music. Make the following announcement:

*Between this session and the next, review the list of optional activities. Do as many of them as you want to.*

Ask the next reader, _____, *will you please read aloud Preparation for the Next Session, on page 49?*

After the section is read, thank the reader and give the following instructions:

*We will finish with our closing song, "I Love Myself," by Jai Josefs. The words are on page 40 of your workbook. Please help put the room back in order before you leave.*

*Now, form a circle, join hands and sing together.*

Play the song on the tape player and sing along. When the song is over, announce:

*Thank you for coming. Our next meeting will be at _____* (place), *at _____* (time and day). *See you next time.*

*Timekeeper's*
*Guide For*

SESSION 5

# LEARNING
# TO ASK

Be sure you have reviewed the information in General Guidelines for the Timekeeper: Sessions 3-14.

Before the meeting, be sure you have the necessary materials:

- Nametags
- Two tapes of background music
- One tape of "The Greatest Love of All"
- One tape of "I Love Myself"
- A timer
- A tape player (be sure you know how to use it)

Arrange the chairs in circles of six facing each other.

Reward promptness by beginning the meeting on time.

*Welcome to the fifth session of Parenting Each Other. My name is _____, and I'm your Timekeeper for this session, Learning to Ask.*

Ask the first reader: _____ *will you please read the commitment statements on page 23?*

177

After the section is read, thank the reader and ask the next reader: _____,
*will you please read the Agreements to Create Safety, Trust and Consistency
on pages 28-29?*

After the section is read, thank the reader and give the following instructions:

*We will start this session with a brief time for sharing. During this time you
may share anything at all with other members of your small group. Remember that there are six people in your small group and only 10 minutes for
sharing, so please be concise.*

*The first person to share will be the person closest to me. You will start by
saying, "What I feel like saying is . . ." and complete a sentence or two about
anything important to you right now. When you are finished, turn to the
person on your right and say, ". . . and that's what I feel like saying. What
do you feel like saying, (Jim, Mary, etc.)?" The next person then says, "What
I feel like saying is . . ." Keep going around the group until I tell you it's time
to stop. If you have nothing to share, say "I pass."*

*You will have 10 mintues to share. I will give you a warning two minutes
before the time is complete. Start now.*

Begin music faintly in the background. Announce the two-minute warning
after eight minutes, and say, *Please stop now* at the end of 10 minutes.

Stop music. Read the introduction to Learning to Ask on page 51. Then
give the following instructions:

*Please take out the Self-Assessment Questionnaires you filled out at Session
1. Use the next three minutes to review your workbook section entitled Self-
Assessment Questionnaire, on page 52.*

Start music. Time for three minutes. Announce when time is up. Give the
following instructions:

*In the first exercise, we'll rehearse asking for what we want as grown-ups.
Please take five minutes to complete Worksheet #11: Not Asking, on page 52.
I'll tell you when the time is up.*

After three minutes, give a two-minute warning. After five minutes say,
*Please stop. Take a minute and read through the instructions for Part 1 of
this exercise on page 52.*

After one minute, say, *Now choose another member of your group as a
partner. Decide who will be the sender and who will be the receiver. Take just
a minute or two for the sender to make a request and for the receiver to
respond.*

At the end of one or two minutes, depending on the noise level in the
room, say, *Now read the instructions for Part 2 of this exercise on page 53.
This should take you about a minute.* After a minute or so, say, *Now, follow
the instructions: the sender makes the request and the receiver responds.
This should take you one to two minutes.*

When the room has quieted down, say, *Please stop. Now take two minutes to share your experience with each other.*

After two minutes, say, *Please stop. Please change roles, review the instructions and repeat both parts of the exercise. When you are through, share your experience with your partner. You will have approximately five minutes to complete this part of the exercise. Start now.*

After three minutes, give a two-minute warning. After five minutes say, *Please stop.*

*Take the next 15 minutes to discuss the questions on page 53 with other members of your small group. Have one person read the question and each member of the group respond to it before moving on to the next question.*

Give a warning after seven minutes. At 13 minutes say, *Two minute warning.* At 15 minutes say, *Please stop now.*

Have all participants take a 10-minute break. At 10 minutes, stop the music and ask participants to form a large circle.

Read the introduction to the Centering Ritual on page 54. Play the tape of "The Greatest Love of All" loudly. Stop the tape promptly when the song is over. Ask participants to return to their group areas. When people are settled, read the following instructions:

*Now prepare to experience what it's like to be three-and-one-half years old and to ask for what you want. Sit quietly with nothing in your lap and follow along with the visualization.*

Play the tape of the visualization or, if you are reading it, play quiet music in the background as you read. Read Slowly! When you have finished the visualization, give the following instructions:

*Take five minutes to write about your experience.* Start music. After five minutes say, *Please stop now.*

*You will have 30 minutes to discuss, in your small group, the answers to the questions on pages 55-56. I will tell you when 15 minutes and 25 minutes have passed, and when to stop.*

Start music. Announce times at 15 minutes and 25 minutes. At 30 minutes, stop the discussion and make the following announcement:

*Take a five-minute break. Then return to your small group and read the instructions for the Nurturing Exchange, on pages 56-57. We will start small group discussion of these instructions in 12 minutes.*

After 12 minutes have passed, announce: *Discuss and clarify the instructions and any reservations you may have in your small group. You will have five minutes for this discussion. If you need more time, please inform the Timekeeper.*

(Timekeeper: you have the option of giving the groups an additional five mintues at this point.) Announce when time is up. Give the following instructions:

*Now choose a partner. Decide which role you will take and proceed with the exchange. I'll give a three-minute warning to put the toys away, and then inform the parenters of the preschoolers when it's time to grow up. I'll tell you when to stop. Begin now.*

At nine minutes, announce the three-minute warning and have the preschoolers put their toys away. At 11 minutes, announce: *Parenters, tell your preschoolers, "It's time to grow up."* At 12 minutes announce:

*Please stop now. Find your workbook and write about your experience for two or three minutes. When you've finished your writing, share your experience with your partner. In seven minutes we will choose new partners and repeat the exercise. Begin writing now.*

At three minutes, announce: *Please share with your partner now.* At seven minutes, announce:

*Please stop. Now choose a new partner who had the opposite role from yours. You will change roles. Review the instructions for your new role. We will start the new Nurturing Exchange in five minutes.*

At five minutes say, *Please begin the Nurturing Exchange. I will tell you when the time is up, as I did before.* Give the three minute warning at nine minutes, and remind the parenters to have the preschoolers put away the toys.

At 11 minutes, announce: *Parenters, it's time to tell your preschoolers to grow up.*

At 12 minutes say, *Please stop now. Find your workbook. Write briefly about your experience and share your experience with your partner. You will have seven minutes to write and share.*

At three minutes announce: *Please begin to share with your partner now.* At five minutes, announce: *You have two minutes left.* At seven minutes, announce: *Please stop now.*

Stop music. Make the following announcement:

*Between this session and the next, review the list of optional activities. Do as many of them as you want to.*

Ask the next reader: _____ *will you please read aloud Preparation for the Next Session, on page 59?* After the section is read, thank the reader and give the following instructions:

*We will finish with our closing song, "I Love Myself," by Jai Josefs. The words are on page 40 of your workbook. Please help put the room back in order before you leave. Now, form a circle, join hands, and sing together.*

Play the song on the tape player and sing along. When the song is over, announce:

*Thank you for coming. Our next meeting will be at _____ (place), at _____ (time and day). See you next time.*

SESSION 6

# HOLDING AND TOUCHING

Be sure you have reviewed the information in General Guidelines for the Timekeeper: Session 3-14.

Before the meeting, be sure you have the necessary materials:

- Nametags
- Two tapes of background music
- One tape of "The Greatest Love of All"
- One tape of "I Love Myself"
- A timer
- A tape player (be sure you know how to use it)

Arrange the chairs in circles of six facing each other.

Reward promptness by beginning the meeting on time.

*Welcome to the sixth session of Parenting Each Other. My name is _____*
*_____ and I'm your Timekeeper for this session,*
*Holding And Touching.*

Ask the first reader: _____, *will you please read the commitment statements on page 23?*

181

After the section is read, thank the reader and ask the next reader: _____
_____, *will you please read the Agreements To Create Safety, Trust And Consistency on pages 28-29?*

After the section is read, thank the reader and give the following instructions:

*We will start this session with a brief time for sharing. During this time you may share anything at all with other members of your small group. Remember that there are six people in your small group and only 10 minutes for sharing, so please be concise.*

*The first person to share will be the person closest to me. You will start by saying, "What I feel like saying is . . ." and complete a sentence or two about anything important to you right now. When you are finished, turn to the person on your right and say, ". . . and that's what I feel like saying. What do you feel like saying, (Jim, Mary, etc.)?" The next person then says, "What I feel like saying is . . ." Keep going around the group until I tell you it's time to stop. If you have nothing to share, say, "I pass."*

*You will have 10 minutes to share. I will give you a warning two mintues before the time is complete. Start now.*

Begin music faintly in the background. Announce the two-minute warning after eight minutes, and say *Please stop now,* at 10 minutes.

Stop music. Read the introduction to Holding And Touching on page 61. Then give the following instructions:

*Please take out the Self-Assessment Questionnaires you filled out at Session 1. Use the next three minutes to review your workbook section entitled Self-Assessment Questionnaire, on page 62.*

Start music. Time for three minutes, and announce when the time is up. Stop music. Have ready the music you will need for this exercise. Use either "The Quiet," by John Michael Talbott, or "Fairy Ring," by Mike Rowland. Play the music at a moderate level throughout the exercise. Ask the first reader:

_____, *will you please read the introduction to the exercise on Silent Appreciation on pages 62-63?*

After the section is read, thank the reader and go on with the exercise. If you have a group of fewer than 12 people, modify the instructions accordingly. Start the music. Signal every two minutes, at an appropriate musical interval, to move to the right. If you wish to participate in this exercise, use a timer that beeps every two minutes. Keep the timer in your hand so it beeps only once.

After 12 minutes, when each person has had the opportunity to face six other people, stop the music and say, *Return to your small groups. You have 15 minutes to discuss the exercise. Use the questions on page 63 to guide your discussion.*

Start a different music tape. At seven minutes say, *Half your time is up.* At 13 minutes, give a two-minute warning, and at 15 minutes, say, *Please stop now.*

Have all participants take a 10-minute break. At 10 minutes, stop the music and ask participants to form a large circle.

Read the introduction to the Centering Ritual on page 63. Play "The Greatest Love of All" loudly. Stop the tape promptly when the song is over. Ask participants to return to their small group areas. When people are settled, read the following instructions:

*Now prepare to experience what it's like to be welcomed to this world as a tiny, tiny baby. Sit quietly with nothing in your lap and follow along with the visualization.*

Play the tape recording of the visualization or, if you are reading it, play quiet music in the background as you read. Read Slowly! When you have finished the visualization, give the following instructions:

*Take five minutes to write about your experience.* Start music. After five minutes say, *Please stop now.*

*You will have 30 minutes to discuss, in your small group, the answers to the questions on page 65. I will tell you when 15 minutes and 25 minutes have passed, and when to stop.*

Start music. Announce times at 15 minutes and 25 minutes. At 30 minutes, stop the discussion and make the following announcement:

*Take a five-minute break. Then return to your small group and read the instructions for the Nurturing Exchange on pages 65-67. We will start small group discussion of these instructions in 12 minutes.*

After 12 minutes have passed, announce: *Discuss and clarify the instructions and any reservations you may have in your small group. You will have five minutes for this discussion. If you need more time, please inform the Timekeeper.*

(Timekeeper: you have the option of giving the groups an additional five minutes at this point.) Announce when time is up. Give the following instructions:

*Now, choose a partner. Decide which role you will take and proceed with the exchange. I'll give a two-minute warning to inform the parenters that it's time to grow up. I'll tell you when to stop. Begin now.*

At eight minutes, announce the two-minute warning. At nine minutes, announce: *Parenters, tell your babies, "It's time to grow up."* The babies will take a minute to get reoriented to being grown-up. At 10 minutes announce:

*Please stop now. Find your workbook and write about your experience of holding or being held. When you've finished your writing, share your experience with your partner. In seven minutes we will choose new partners and repeat the exercise. Begin writing now.*

At three minutes, announce: *Please share with your partner now.* At seven minutes, announce:

*Please stop. Now, choose a new partner who had the opposite role from yours. You will change roles. Review the instructions for your new role. We will start the new Nurturing Exchange in five minutes.*

At five minutes say, *Please begin the Nurturing Exchange. I will tell you when the time is up, as I did before.* Give the two-minute warning at eight minutes. At nine minutes, announce: *Parenters, it's time to tell your babies to grow up.*

Give the babies a minute to get reoriented to being grown-up.

At 10 minutes say, *Please stop now. Find your workbook. Write briefly about your experience and share your experience with your partner. You will have seven minutes to write and share.*

At five minutes, announce: *You have two minutes left.* At seven minutes, annouce: *Please stop now.*

Stop music. Make the following announcement:

*Between this session and the next, review the list of optional activities. Do as many of them as you want to.*

_____, *will you please read aloud Preparation for the Next Session, on page 68?*

After the section is read, thank the reader and give the following instructions:

*We will finish with our closing song, "I Love Myself," by Jai Josefs. The words are on page 40 of your workbook. Please help put the room back in order before you leave.*

*Now, form a circle, join hands, and sing together.*

Play the song on the tape player and sing along. When the song is over, announce:

*Thank you for coming. Our next meeting will be at* _____ (place), *at* _____ (time and day). *See you next time.*

*Timekeeper's
Guide For*

SESSION 7

# ASKING FOR
# CLOSENESS

Be sure you have reviewed the information in General Guidelines for the Timekeeper: Sessions 3-14.

Before the meeting, be sure you have the necessary materials:

- Nametags
- Two tapes of background music
- One tape of "The Greatest Love of All"
- One tape of "I Love Myself"
- A timer
- A tape player (be sure you know how to use it)

Arrange the chairs in circles of six facing each other.

Reward promptness by beginning the meeting on time.

*Welcome to the seventh session of Parenting Each Other. My name is
_____, and I'm your Timekeeper for this session,
Asking For Closeness.*

*Ask the first reader:* _____, *will you please
read the commitment statements, on page 23?*

After the section is read, thank the reader and ask the next reader: _____
_____, *will you please read the Agreements to Create Safety, Trust, and Consistency, on pages 28-29?*

After the section is read, thank the reader and give the following instructions:

*We will start this session with a brief time for sharing. During this time you may share anything at all with other members of your small group. Remember that there are six people in your small group and only 10 minutes for sharing, so please be concise.*

*The first person to share will be the person closest to me. You will start by saying, "What I feel like saying is . . ." and complete a sentence or two about anything important to you right now. When you are finished, turn to the person on your right and say, ". . . and that's what I feel like saying. What do you feel like saying, (Jim, Mary, etc.)?" The next person then says, "What I feel like saying is . . ." Keep going around the group until I tell you it's time to stop. If you have nothing to share, say, "I pass."*

*Take five minutes to write about your experience.* Start music. After five minutes say, *Please stop now.*

Begin music faintly in the background. Announce the two-minute warning after eight minutes, and say *Please stop now* at 10 minutes.

Stop music. Read the introduction to Asking For Closeness on page 71. Then give the following instructions:

*Please take out the Self-Assessment Questionnaire you filled out at Session 1. Use the next three minutes to review your workbook section entitled Self-Assessment Questionnaire, on page 72.*

Start music. Time for three minutes. Announce when the time is up. Give the following instructions:

*Please turn to Worksheet #12: Engulfment And Abandonment, on pages 72-73. You will have eight minutes to complete it. I will warn you when two minutes remain.*

Announce when four minutes have passed. When six minutes have passed say, *Two-minute warning.* When eight minutes have passed, say, *Please stop now.*

*Now take 15 minutes to share your answers in your small group. Each person shares the answer to the first question before moving on to the second question. Then discuss the answers to the rest of the questions in your workbook. Begin now.*

Tell the group when seven minutes have passed. At 13 minutes say, *Two-minute warning.* At 15 minutes say, *Please stop now.*

Have all participants take a 10-minute break. At 10 minutes, stop the music and ask participants to form a large circle.

Read the introduction to the Centering Ritual on page 73. Play the tape "The Greatest Love of All" loudly. Stop the tape promptly when the song is over. Ask participants to return to their small group areas. When people are settled, read the following instructions:

*Now prepare to experience what it's like to be Jackie, a 20-month-old explorer who is parented appropriately with love, support and appropriate limits. Sit quietly with nothing in your lap and follow along with the visualization.*

Play the tape recording of the visualization or, if you are reading it, play quiet music in the background as you read. Read Slowly! When you have finished the visualization, give the following instructions:

*Take five minutes to write about your experience.* Start music. After five minutes say, *Please stop now.*

*You will have 30 minutes to discuss, in your small group, the answers to the questions on page 75. I will tell you when 15 minutes and 25 minutes have passed, and when to stop.*

Start music. Announce times at 15 minutes and 25 minutes. At 30 minutes, stop the discussion and and make the following announcement:

*Take a five-minute break. Then return to your small group and read the instructions for the Nurturing Exchange, on pages 75-77. We will start small group discussion of these instructions in 12 minutes.*

After 12 minutes have passed, announce: *Discuss and clarify the instructions and any reservations you may have in your small group. You will have five minutes for this discussion. If you need more time, please inform the Timekeeper.*

(Timekeeper: you have the option of giving the groups an additional five minutes at this point.) Announce when time is up. Give the following instructions:

*Now, choose a partner. Decide which role you will take and proceed with the exchange. I'll give a two-minute warning to inform the parenters of the toddlers when it's time to grow up. I'll tell you when to stop. Begin now.*

At 10 minutes, announce the two-minute warning. At 11 minutes, announce: *Parenters, tell your toddlers, "It's time to grow up."* The toddlers will take a minute to get reoriented to being grown up. At 12 minutes, announce:

*Please stop now. Find your workbook and write about your experience. When you've finished your writing, share your experience with your partner. In seven minutes we will choose new partners and repeat the exercise. Begin writing now.*

At three minutes, announce: *Please share with your partner now.* At seven minutes, announce:

*Please stop. Now, choose a new partner who had the opposite role from yours. You will change roles. Review the instructions for your new role. We will start the new Nurturing Exchange in five minutes.*

At five minutes say: *Please begin the Nurturing Exchange. I will tell you when the time is up, as I did before.* Give the two-minute warning at 10 minutes. At 11 minutes, announce: *Parenters, it's time to tell your toddlers to grow up.*

Give the toddlers a minute to get reoriented to being grown up. At 12 minutes say, *Please stop now.*

*Find your workbook. Write briefly about your experience and share your experience with your partner. You will have seven minutes to write and share.*

At five minutes, announce: *You have two minutes left.* At seven minutes, announce: *Please stop now.*

Stop music. Make the following announcement:

*Between this session and the next, review the list of optional activities. Do as many of them as you want to.*

_____, *will you please read aloud Preparation for the Next Session, on page 78?*

After the section is read, thank the reader and give the following instructions:

*We will finish with our closing song, "I Love Myself," by Jai Josefs. The words are on page 40 of your workbook. Please help put the room back in order before you leave.*

*Now, form a circle, join hands, and sing together.*

Play the song on the tape player and sing along. When the song is over, announce:

*Thank you for coming. Our next meeting will be at _____* (place), *at _____* (time and day). *See you next time.*

*Timekeeper's*
*Guide For*

# WHY? WHY? WHY?

Be sure you have reviewed the information in General Guidelines for the Timekeeper: Sessions 3-14.

Before the meeting, be sure you have the necessary materials:

- Nametags
- Two tapes of background music
- One tape of "The Greatest Love of All"
- One tape of "I Love Myself"
- A timer
- A tape player (be sure you know how to use it)

Arrange the chairs in circles of six facing each other.

Reward promptness by beginning the meeting on time.

*Welcome to the eighth session of Parenting Each Other. My name is* _____
_____, *and I'm your Timekeeper for this session, Why? Why? Why?*

Ask the first reader: _____, *will you please read the commitment statements, on page 23?*

After the section is read, thank the reader and ask the next reader: _____
_____, *will you please read the*
*Agreements to Create Safety, Trust, and Consistency, on pages 28-29?*

After the section is read, thank the reader and give the following instructions:

*We will start this session with a brief time for sharing. During this time you may share anything at all with other members of your small group. Remember that there are six people in your small group and only 10 minutes for sharing, so please be concise.*

*The first person to share will be the person closest to me. You will start by saying, "What I feel like saying is . . ." and complete a sentence or two about anything important to you right now. When you have finished, turn to the person on your right and say, ". . . and that's what I feel like saying. What do you feel like saying, (Jim, Mary, etc.)?" The next person then says, "What I feel like saying is . . ." Keep going around the group until I tell you it's time to stop. If you have nothing to share, say, "I pass."*

*You will have 10 minutes to share. I will give you a warning two minutes before the time is complete. Start now.*

Begin music faintly in the background. Announce the two-minute warning after eight minutes, and say, *Please stop now* at the end of 10 minutes.

Stop music. Read the introduction to Why? Why? Why? on page 81. Then give the following instructions:

*Please take out the Self-Assessment Questionnaires you filled out at Session 1. Use the next three minutes to review your workbook section entitled Self-Assessment Questionnaire on page 81.*

Start music. Time for three minutes. Announce when time is up. Give the following instructions:

*Please take five minutes to complete Worksheet #13: Questions, on page 82. Begin now.*

When three minutes have passed, say, *Two-minute warning.* When five minutes have passed, say, *Please stop now.*

Stop music. Read the first two paragraphs of the exercise instructions on page 82 aloud. Say, *You have 12 minutes to answer each other's questions. Start now.*

Start music. Tell the group when six minutes have passed. At 10 minutes say, *Two-minute warning.*

At 12 minutes say, *Please stop now. Now take three minutes or so to write about your experience of both asking and answering these questions. Begin now.*

When three minutes are up, announce, *Your time is up. Please stop now. Spend a few minutes sharing with your partners how you felt about asking and answering the questions. You have five minutes.*

Give a two-minute warning at three minutes. At five minutes, announce, *Please stop now.*

Have all participants take a 10-minute break. At 10 minutes, stop the music and ask participants to form a large circle.

Read the introduction to the Centering Ritual. Play the tape of "The Greatest Love of All" loudly. Stop the tape promptly when the song is over. Ask participants to return to their small group areas. When people are settled, read the following instructions:

*Now prepare to experience what it's like to have the normal behaviors of a curious four-year-old child responded to appropriately with love, support and appropriate answers. Sit quietly with nothing in your lap and follow along with the visualization.*

Play the tape recording of the visualization or, if you are reading it, play quiet music in the background as you read. Read Slowly! When you have finished the visualization, give the following instructions:

*Take five minutes to write about your experience.* Start music. After five minutes say, *Please stop now.*

*You will have 30 minutes to discuss, in your small group, the answers to the questions on page 85. I will tell you when 15 minutes and 25 minutes have passed, and when to stop.*

Start music. Announce times at 15 minutes and 25 minutes. At 30 minutes, stop the discussion and make the following announcement:

*Take a five-minute break. Then return to your group and read the instructions for the Nurturing Exchange on pages 85-87. We will start small group discussion of these instructions in 12 minutes.*

After 12 minutes have passed, announce: *Discuss and clarify the instructions and any reservations you may have in your small group. You will have five minutes for this discussion. If you need more time, please inform the Timekeeper.*

(Timekeeper: you have the option of giving the groups an additional five minutes at this point.) Announce when time is up. Give the following instructions:

*Now, choose a partner. Decide which role you will take, and proceed with the exchange. I'll give a two-minute warning to inform the parenters of the four-year-olds that it's time to grow up. I'll tell you when to stop. Begin now.*

At 10 minutes, announce the two-minute warning. At 11 minutes, announce: *Parenters, tell your four-year-olds, "It's time to grow up."* At 12 minutes, announce:

*Please stop now. Find your workbook and write about your experience for two or three minutes. When you've finished your writing, share your experience with your partner. In seven minutes we will choose new partners and repeat the exercise. Begin writing now.*

At three minutes, announce: *Please share with your partner now.* At seven minutes, announce:

*Please stop. Now choose a new partner who had the opposite role from yours. You will change roles. Review the instructions for your new role. We will start the new Nurturing Exchange in five minutes.*

At five minutes say, *Please begin the Nurturing Exchange. I will tell you when the time is up, as I did before.* Give the two-minute warning at 10 minutes. At 11 minutes, announce: *Parenters, it's time to tell your four-year-olds to grow up.*

At 12 minutes say, *Please stop now. Find your workbook. Write briefly about your experience and share your experience with your partner. You will have seven minutes to write and share.*

At three minutes announce: *Please begin to share with your partner now.* At seven minutes, announce: *Please stop now.*

Stop music. Make the following announcement:

*Between this session and the next, review the list of optional activities. Do as many of them as you want to.*

_____, *will you please read aloud Preparation for the Next Session, on page 88?*

After the section is read, thank the reader and give the following instructions:

*We will finish with our closing song, "I Love Myself," by Jai Josefs. The words are on page 40 of your workbook. Please help put the room back in order before you leave.*

*Now, form a circle, join hands, and sing together.*

Play the song on the tape player and sing along. When the song is over, announce:

*Thank you for coming. Our next meeting will be at* _____ (place), *at* _____ (time and day). *See you next time.*

*Timekeeper's*
*Guide For*

# JUST HOW POWERFUL AM I?

Be sure you have reviewed the information in General Guidelines for the Timekeeper: Sessions 3-14.

Before the meeting, be sure you have the necessary materials:

- Nametags
- Two tapes of background music
- One tape of "The Greatest Love of All"
- One tape of "I Love Myself"
- A timer
- A tape player (be sure you know how ot use it)

Arrange the chairs in circles of six facing each other.

Reward promptness by beginning the meeting on time.

*Welcome to the ninth session of Parenting Each Other. My name is* _____
_____, *and I'm your Timekeeper for this session, Just How Powerful Am I.*

Ask the first reader: _____, *will you please read the commitment statements, on page 23?*

After the section is read, thank the reader and ask the next reader: _____
_____, *will you please read the*
*Agreements to Create Safety, Trust, and Consistency, on pages 28-29?*
After the section is read, thank the reader and give the following instructions:

*We will start this session with a brief time for sharing. During this time you*
*may share anything at all with other members of your small group. Remem-*
*ber that there are six people in your small group and only 10 minutes for*
*sharing, so please be concise.*

*The first person to share will be the person closest to me. You will start by*
*saying, "What I feel like saying is . . ." and complete a sentence or two about*
*anything important to your right now. When you are finished, turn to the*
*person on your right and say, ". . . and that's what I feel like saying. What*
*do you feel like saying, (Jim, Mary, etc.)?" The next person then says, "What*
*I feel like saying is . . ." Keep going around the group until I tell you it's time*
*to stop. If you have nothing to share, say, "I pass."*

*You will have 10 minutes to share. I will give you a warning two minutes*
*before the time is complete. Start now.*

Begin music faintly in the background. Announce the two-minute warning
after eight minutes, and say *Please stop now,* at the end of 10 minutes.

Stop music. Read the introduction to Just How Powerful Am I? on page 89.
Then give the following instructions:

*Please take out the Self-Assessment Questionnaire you filled out at Session*
*1. Use the next three minutes to review your workbook section entitled Self-*
*Assessment Questionnaire on page 90.*

Start music. Time for three minutes. Announce when time is up. Give the
following instructions:

*Please take seven minutes to complete Worksheet #14: Who Makes Whom*
*Feel What, on pages 90-91.*

When five minutes have passed, say, *Two-minute warning.* When seven
minutes have passed say, *Please stop now.*

Stop music. Then give the following instructions:

*The instructions for the exercise are on pages 91-92. Let each person in*
*your small group take up to one minute to share their own insights gained*
*from filling out the Worksheet. Then discuss the questions that are in your*
*workbook. You'll have a total of 20 minutes for this part of the exercise.*
*Discuss as many questions as you have time for. Don't worry if you don't*
*answer them all. Start now.*

Start music. At six minutes, say, *Six minutes are up; you should be done*
*with your individual sharing and moving on to the questions now.* At 12
minutes, say, *You have eight minutes left.* At 18 minutes, say, *You have two*
*minutes left.* At 20 minutes, say, *Please stop now.*

Have all participants take a 10-minute break. At 10 minutes stop the music and ask participants to form a large circle.

Read the introduction to the Centering Ritual on page 92. Play the tape of "The Greatest Love of All" loudly. Stop the tape promptly when the song is over. Ask participants to return to their small group area. When people are settled, read the first two paragraphs that introduce the visualization on page 92, and give the following instructions:

*Now, prepare to experience what it's like to be four years old and learning from a wise and loving grandmother how you can have an effective impact on the world. Sit quietly with nothing in your lap and follow along with the visualization.*

Play the tape recording of the visualizations or, if you are reading it, play quiet music in the background as you read. Read Slowly! When you have finished the visualization, give the following instructions:

*Take five minutes to write about your experience.* Start music. After five minutes say, *Please stop now.*

*You will have 30 minutes to discuss, in your small group, the answers to the questions beginning on page 93. I will tell you when 15 minutes and 25 minutes have passed, and when to stop.*

Start music. Announce times at 15 minutes and 25 minutes. At 30 minutes, stop the discussion and make the following announcement:

*Take a five-minute break. Then return to your small group and read the instructions for the Nurturing Exchange on pages 94-96. We will start small group discussion of these instructions in 12 minutes.*

After 12 minutes have passed, announce: *Discuss and clarify the instructions and any reservations you may have in your small group. You will have five minutes for this discussion. If you need more time, please inform the Timekeeper.*

(Timekeeper: you have the option of giving the groups an additional five minutes at this point.) Announce when time is up. Give the following instructions:

*Now choose a partner. Decide which role you will take and proceed with the exchange. I'll give a two-minute warning to inform the parenters of the four-year-olds that it's time to grow up. I'll tell you when to stop. Begin now.*

At eight minutes, announce the two-minute warning. At nine minutes, announce: *Parenters, tell your four-year-olds, "It's time to grow up."* At 10 minutes, announce:

*Please stop now. Find your workbook and write about your experience for two or three minutes. When you've finished writing, share your experience with your partner. In seven minutes we will choose new partners and repeat the exercise. Begin writing now.*

At three minutes, announce: *Please share with your partner now.* At seven minutes, announce:

*Please stop. Now, choose a new partner who had the opposite role from yours. You will change roles. Review the instructions for your new role. We will start the new Nurturing Exchange in five minutes.*

At five minutes say, *Please begin the Nurturing Exchange. I will tell you when the time is up, as I did before.* Give the two-minute warning at eight minutes. At nine minutes, announce: *Parenters, it's time to tell your four-year-olds to grow up.*

At 10 minutes say, *Please stop now. Find your workbook. Write briefly about your experience and share your experience with your partner. You will have seven minutes to write and share.*

At four minutes announce: *Please begin to share with your partner now.* At seven minutes, announce: *Please stop now.*

Stop music. Make the following announcement.

*Between this session and the next, review the list of optional activities. Do as many of them as you want to.*

_____, *will you please read aloud Preparation for the Next Session, on pages 97-98?*

After the section is read, thank the reader and give the following instructions:

*We will finish with our closing song, "I Love Myself," by Jai Josefs. The words are on page 40 of your workbook. Please help put the room back in order before you leave.*

Play the song on the tape player and sing along. When the song is over, announce:

*Thank you for coming. Our next meeting will be at _____ (place), at _____ (time and day). See you next time.*

*Timekeeper's*
*Guide For*

SESSION 10

# MAKING MISTAKES IS OKAY

Be sure you have reviewed the information in General Guidelines for the Timekeeper: Sessions 3-14.

Before the meeting, be sure you have the necessary materials:

- Nametags
- Two tapes of background music
- One tape of "The Greatest Love of All"
- ·One tape of "I Love Myself"
- A timer
- A tape player (be sure you know how to use it)

Arrange the chairs in circles of six facing each other.

Reward promptness by beginning the meeting on time.

*Welcome to the tenth session of Parenting Each Other. My name is* _____
_____, *and I'm your Timekeeper*
*for this session, Making Mistakes Is Okay.*

Ask the first reader: _____, *will you please read*
*the commitment statements, on page 23?*

197

After the section is read, thank the reader and ask the next reader: _____
_____, *will you please read the*
*Agreements to Create Safety, Trust, and Consistency, on pages 28-29?*

*We will start this session with a brief time for sharing. During this time you*
*may share anything at all with other members of your small group. Remem-*
*ber that there are six people in your small group and only 10 minutes for*
*sharing, so please be concise.*

*The first person to share will be the person closest to me. You may start by*
*saying, "What I feel like saying is . . ." and complete a sentence or two about*
*anything important to you right now. When you are finished, turn to the*
*person on your right and say, ". . . and that's what I feel like saying. What*
*do you feel like saying, (Jim, Mary, etc.)?" The next person then says, "What*
*I feel like saying is . . ." Keep going around the group until I tell you it's time*
*to stop. If you have nothing to share, say, "I pass."*

*You will have 10 minutes to share. I will give you a warning two minutes*
*before the time is complete. Start now.*

Begin music faintly in the background. Announce the two-minute warning
after eight minutes, and say *Please stop now* at the end of 10 minutes.

Stop music. Read the instructions to Making Mistakes Is Okay, on page 99.
Then give the following instructions:

*Please take out the Self-Assessment Questionnaires you filled out at Session*
*1. Use the next three minutes to review your workbook section entitled Self-*
*Assessment Questionnaire, on page 99.*

Start music. Time for three minutes. Announce when time is up. Give the
following instructions:

*Please take five minutes to complete Worksheet #15: Mistakes, on page*
*100. Begin now.*

When three minutes have passed, say, *Two-minute warning.* When five
minutes have passed, say, *Please stop now.*

Stop music. Then give the following instructions:

*Read the instructions for the exercise on page 100. You'll have 15 minutes*
*to discuss this Worksheet in your small group. Each of you take a minute or*
*two to describe your recent mistake and your answers to Questions 1 through*
*8. Remember to be supportive of each other. After each person has described*
*their answers to the first eight questions, then each one take a turn sharing*
*your answers to Questions 9, 10 and 11.*

Start music. At seven minutes, announce that seven minutes have passed.
At 13 minutes, say, *You have two minutes left.* At 15 minutes, say, *Please stop*
*now.*

Have all participants take a 10-minute break. At 10 minutes, stop the music
and ask participants to form a large circle.

Read the introduction to the Centering Ritual on page 101. Play the tape of "The Greatest Love of All" loudly. Stop the tape promptly when the song is over. Ask the participants to return to their small group area. When people are settled, read the paragraphs that introduce the visualization on page 101 and give the following instructions:

*Now, prepare to experience what it's like to be Ronnie and learning that making mistakes is okay. Sit quietly with nothing in your lap and follow along with the visualization.*

Play the tape recording of the visualization or, if you are reading it, play quiet music in the background as you read. Read Slowly! When you have finished the visualization, give the following instructions:

*Take five minutes to write about your experience.* Start music. After five minutes say, *Please stop now.*

*You will have 30 minutes to discuss, in your small group, the answers to the questions on pages 103-104. I will tell you when 15 minutes and 25 minutes have passed, and when to stop.*

Start music. Announce times at 15 minutes and 25 minutes. At 30 minutes, stop the discussion and make the following announcement:

*Take a five-minute break. Then return to your small group and read the instructions for the Nurturing Exchange, on pages 104-106. We will start small group discussion of these instructions in 12 minutes.*

After 12 minutes have passed, announce: *Discuss and clarify the instructions and any reservations you may have in your small group. You will have five minutes for this discussion.*

Announce when time is up. Divide the group into learners and teachers. You can have them count off ("One, two, one, two, etc."), or simply draw a line across the group and say, This side is the learners and this side is the teachers. Give the following instructions:

*Each learner tells the entire group what skill you would like to learn using materials you brought with you. Say, "I would like to learn to knit, build a model airplane, work a yo-yo, play jacks, etc." If you can teach a skill someone else wants to learn, raise your hand so the learner knows you would make a suitable partner.*

Ask each learner to say what s/he would like to learn. Call on each in turn. Then say:

*Learners, find a partner who can teach you what you want to learn. The teacher is a resource for you. You need to be responsible for your own learning. One teacher may assist more than one learner at a time. You will have 10 minutes for the teaching/learning experience. I'll give you a two-minute warning. Begin now.*

Start music. At eight minutes, announce a two-minute warning. At 10 minutes, announce, *Please stop now.*

*Find your workbook and write about your experience. When you've finished writing, share your experience with your partner. In seven minutes, we will choose new partners and repeat the exercise. Begin writing now.*

At three minutes announce: *Please share with your partner now.* At seven minutes, announce, *Please stop now.*

*Find a new partner. Teachers, become learners. New learners, tell the entire group what you would like to learn, as before. Choose appropriate teachers for yourselves. You will have 10 minutes for the teaching/learning experience. Review the instructions for your new role. We will start the new Nurturing Exchange in five minutes.*

Start music. At five minutes say, *Please begin the Nurturing Exchange. I will give you a two-minute warning, and tell you when the time is up, as I did before.*

At eight minutes, announce a two-minute warning. At 10 minutes, announce, *Please stop now. Find your workbook and write about your experience. When you've finished writing, share your experience with your partner. Begin writing now.*

At three minutes, announce, *Please share with your partner now.* At seven minutes, announce, *Please stop now.*

If there are 20 minutes left before the session is scheduled to close, give the following instructions for an optional exercise:

*Please return to your small group and share the answers to the questions at the end of the Doing It section on page 106 in your workbook. You have 10 minutes. Begin now.*

At eight minutes, give a two-minute warning. At 10 minutes, say, *Please stop now.* Stop music. Make the following announcements:

*Between this session and the next, review the list of optional activities. Do as many activities as you want to.*

*There are no special materials necessary for the next session.*

*We will finish with our closing song, "I Love Myself," by Jai Josefs. The words are on page 40 of your workbook. Please help put the room back in order before you leave.*

*Now, form a circle, join hands, and sing together.*

Play the song on the tape player and sing along. When the song is over, announce:

*Thank you for coming. Our next meeting will be at _____ (place), at _____ (time and day). See you next time.*

*Timekeeper's*
*Guidelines For*

# NEGOTIATION SKILLS

Be sure you have reviewed the information in General Guidelines for the Timekeeper: Sessions 3-14.

Before the meeting, be sure you have the necessary materials:

- Nametags
- Two tapes of background music
- One tape of "The Greatest Love of All"
- One tape of "I Love Myself"
- A timer
- A tape player (be sure you know how to use it)

Arrange the chairs in circles of six facing each other.

Reward promptness by beginning the meeting on time.

*Welcome to the eleventh session of Parenting Each Other. My name is* _____, *and I'm your Timekeeper for this session, Negotiation Skills.*

Ask the first reader: _____, *will you please read the commitment statements on page 23?*

201

After the section is read, thank the reader and ask the next reader: _____
_____, *will you please read the*
*Agreements to Create Safety, Trust, and Consistency, on pages 28-29?*

After the section is read, thank the reader and give the following instructions:

*We will start this session with a brief time for sharing. During this time you*
*may share anything at all with other members of your small group. Remem-*
*ber that there are six people in your small group and only 10 minutes for*
*sharing, so please be concise.*

*The first person to share will be the person closest to me. You will start by*
*saying, "What I feel like saying is . . ." and complete a sentence or two about*
*anything important to you right now. When you are finished, turn to the*
*person on your right and say, ". . . and that's what I feel like saying. What*
*do you feel like saying, (Jim, Mary, etc)?" The next person then says, "What*
*I feel like saying is . . ." Keep going around the group until I tell you it's time*
*to stop. If you have nothing to share, say, "I pass."*

*You will have 10 minutes to share. I will give you a warning two minutes*
*before the time is complete. Start now.*

Begin music faintly in the background. Announce the two-minute warning
after eight minutes, and say *Please stop now,* at the end of 10 minutes.

Stop music. Read the introduction to Negotiation Skills, on page 109. Then
give the following instructions:

*Please take out the Self-Assessment Questionnaires you filled out at Session*
*1. Use the next three mintues to review your workbook section entitled Self-*
*Assessment Questionnaire, on page 110.*

Start music. Time for three minutes. Announce when time is up. Give the
following instructions:

*Please take 10 minutes to complete Worksheet #16: Conflict, on pages 110-*
*111.*

At five minutes, say, *Half the time is up.* At eight minutes, announce, *You*
*have two minutes left.* At 10 minutes, announce, *Please stop now.*

Stop music. Then give the following instructions:

*Now, briefly share your answers to Questions 1 through 8 in your small*
*group, giving each person the opportunity to answer Question 1 before going*
*on to Question 2, etc. When you get to Question 9, you may want to spend*
*a little more time discussing it. You have 15 minutes for your discussion. I'll*
*warn you when half the time is up.*

Start music. At seven minutes, say, *Half the time is up.* At 13 minutes,
announce a two-minute warning. At 15 minutes, say, *Please stop.*

Have all participants take a 10-minute break. At 10 minutes, stop the music
and ask participants to form a large circle.

Read the introduction to the Centering Ritual on pages 111-112. Play the tape of "The Greatest Love of All" loudly. Stop the tape promptly when the song is over. Have the participants return to their small group area. When they are settled, read the introductory paragraphs of the Negotiation Skills visualization on page 112, and give the following instructions:

*Now, prepare to experience what it's like to be an eleven-year-old who is successfully practicing the negotiation skills learned during the last five or six years. Sit quietly with nothing in your lap and follow along with the visualization.*

Play the tape recording of the visualization or, if you are reading it, play quiet music in the background as you read. Read Slowly! When you have finished the visualization, give the following instructions:

*Take five minutes to write about your experience.* Start music. After five minutes say, *Please stop now.*

*You will have 30 minutes to discuss, in your small group, the answers to the questions on pages 113. I will tell you when 15 minutes and 25 minutes have passed, and when to stop.*

Start music. Announce times at 15 minutes and 25 minutes. At 30 minutes, stop the discussion and make the following announcement:

*Take a five-minute break. Then return to your small group and read the instructions for the Nurturing Exchange, on pages 113-115. We will start small group discussion of these instructions in 10 minutes.*

After 10 minutes have passed, announce: *Discuss and clarify the instructions and any reservations you may have in your small group. You will have five minutes for this discussion. If you need more time, please inform the Timekeeper.*

(Timekeeper: you have the option of giving the groups an additional five minutes at this point.) Announce when time is up. Give the following instructions:

*Now, choose a partner. Decide which role you will take and proceed with the exchange. I'll give a two-minute warning to inform the parenters of the eleven-year-olds that it's time to grow up. I'll tell you when to stop. Begin now.*

At eight minutes, announce the two-minute warning. At nine minutes, announce: *Parenters, tell your school-age children, "It's time to grow up."* At 10 minutes announce:

*Please stop now. Find your workbook and write about your experience for two or three minutes. When you've finished writing, share your experience with your partner. In seven minutes we will choose new partners and repeat the exercise. Begin writing now.*

At three minutes, announce: *Please share with your partner now.* At seven minutes, announce:

*Please stop. Now, choose a new partner who had the opposite role from yours. You will change roles. Review the instructions for your new role. We will start the new Nurturing Exchange in five minutes.*

At five minutes say, *Please begin the Nurturing Exchange. I will tell you when the time is up, as I did before.*

Give the two-minute warning at eight minutes. At nine minutes, announce: *Parenters, it's time to tell your school-age children to grow up.*

At 10 minutes say, *Please stop now. Find your workbook. Write briefly about your experience and share your experience with your partner. You will have seven minutes to write and share.*

At three minutes announce: *Please begin to share with your partner now.* At seven minutes, announce: *Please stop now.*

Stop music. Make the following announcement:

*Between this session and the next, review the list of optional activities. Do as many of them as you want to.*

_____, *will you please read aloud Preparation for the Next Session on page 116?*

After the section is read, thank the reader and give the following instructions:

*We will finish with our closing song, "I Love Myself," by Jai Josefs. The words are on page 40 of your workbook. Please help put the room back in order before you leave.*

*Now, form a circle, join hands, and sing together.*

Play the song on the tape player and sing along. When the song is over, announce:

*Thank you for coming. Our next meeting will be at _____ (place), at _____ (time and day). See you next time.*

*Timekeeper's*
*Guide For*

# MORE ABOUT BOUNDARIES

Be sure you have reviewed the information in General Guidelines for the Timekeeper: Sessions 3-14.

Before the meeting, be sure you have the necessary materials:

- Nametags
- Two tapes of background music
- One tape of "The Greatest Love of All"
- One tape of "I Love Myself"
- A timer
- A tape player (be sure you know how to use it)

Arrange the chairs in circles of six facing each other.

Reward promptness by beginning the meeting on time.

*Welcome to the twelfth session of Parenting Each Other. My name is* _____, *and I'm your Timekeeper for this session, More About Boundaries.*

Ask the first reader: _____, *will you please read the commitment statements on page 23?*

205

After the section is read, thank the reader and ask the next reader: _____
_____, *will you please read the*
*Agreements To Create Safety, Trust And Consistency on pages 28-29?*

After the section is read, thank the reader and give the following instructions:

*We will start this session with a brief time for sharing. During this time you*
*may share anything at all with other members of your small group. Remember that there are six people in your small group and only 10 minutes for*
*sharing, so please be concise.*

*The first person to share will be the person closest to me. You will start by*
*saying, "What I feel like saying is . . ." and complete a sentence or two about*
*anything important to you right now. When you are finished, turn to the*
*person on your right and say, ". . . and that's what I feel like saying. What*
*do you feel like saying, (Jim, Mary, etc.)?" The next person then says, "What*
*I feel like saying is . . ." Keep going around the group until I tell you it's time*
*to stop. If you have nothing to share, say, "I pass."*

*You will have 10 minutes to share. I will give you a warning two minutes*
*before the time is complete. Start now.*

Begin music faintly in the background. Announce the two-minute warning
after eight minutes, and say *Please stop now,* at 10 minutes.

Stop music. Read the introduction to More About Boundaries on page 117.
Then give the following instructions:

*Please take out the Self-Assessment Questionnaires you filled out at Session*
*1. Use the next three minutes to review your workbook section entitled Self-*
*Assessment Questionnaire, on page 117.*

Start music. Time for three minutes. Announce when time is up. Give the
following instructions:

*Please take eight minutes to complete Worksheet #17: Boundaries, on*
*pages 118-119.*

At four minutes, announce, *Half the time is up.* At six minutes announce,
*You have two minutes left.* At eight minutes, announce, *Please stop now.* Stop
music. Then give the following instructions:

*The instructions for the exercise are on page 119. Let each person in your*
*small group take up to one minute to share their own insights gained from*
*filling out the Worksheet. Then discuss the questions that are in your work-*
*book. You'll have a total of 20 minutes for this part of the exercise. Discuss*
*as many questions as you have time for. Don't worry if you don't answer*
*them all. There are no right answers in any of these situations. The objective*
*of the sharing is to find out what your limits are, and how they are like or*
*unlike other people's limits. This will give you more information and suggest*
*other areas in which change is possible. Discuss each person's response to one*

*situation before you go on to the next situation. I'll inform you when 10 minutes have passed and give you a two-minute warning. Start now.*

At 10 minutes, say, *Ten minutes are up.* At 18 minutes, say, *You have two minutes left.* At 20 minutes, say, *Please stop now.*

Have all participants take a 10-minute break. At 10 minutes, stop the music and ask participants to form a large circle.

Read the introduction to the Centering Ritual on page 119. Play the tape of "The Greatest Love of All" loudly. Stop the tape promptly when the song is over.

Have the participants return to their small group area. When they are settled, give the following instructions:

*Now prepare to experience what it's like to be a 13-year-old whose Dad is insisting that you learn to be responsible for keeping the agreements you make. Sit quietly with nothing in your lap and follow along with the visualization.*

Play the tape recording of the visualization or, if you are reading it, play quiet music in the background as you read. Read Slowly! When you have finished the visualization, give the following instructions:

*Take five minutes to write about your experience.* Start music. After five minutes say, *Please stop now.*

*You will have 30 minutes to discuss, in your small group, the answers to the questions on page 121. I will tell you when 15 minutes and 25 minutes have passed, and when to stop.*

Start music. Announce times at 15 minutes and 25 minutes. At 30 minutes, stop the discussion and make the following announcement:

*Take a five-minute break. Then return to your small group and read the instructions for the Nurturing Exchange, on pages 122-124. We will start small group discussion of these instructions in 12 minutes.*

After 12 minutes have passed, announce: *Discuss and clarify the instructions and any reservations you may have in your small group. You will have five minutes for this discussion. If you need more time, please inform the Timekeeper.*

(Timekeeper: you have the option of giving the groups an additional five minutes at this point.) Announce when time is up. Give the following instructions:

*Now, choose a partner. Decide which role you will take and proceed with the exchange. I'll give a two-minute warning, and I'll tell you when to stop. Begin now.*

At eight minutes, announce the two-minute warning. At 10 minutes, announce: *Please stop now. Find your workbook and write about your experience for two or three minutes. When you've finished writing, share your experience with your partner. In seven minutes we will choose new partners and repeat the exercise. Begin writing now.*

At three minutes, announce: *Please share with your partner now.* At seven minutes, announce:

*Please stop. Now, choose a new partner who had the opposite role from yours. You will change roles. Review the instructions for your new role. We will start the new Nurturing Exchange in five minutes.*

At five minutes say, *Please begin the Nurturing Exchange. I will tell you when the time is up, as I did before.* Give the two-minute warning at eight minutes. At 10 minutes say, *Please stop now.*

*Find your workbook. Write briefly about your experience and share your experience with your partner. You will have seven minutes to write and share.*

At three minutes announce: *Please begin to share with your partner now.* At seven minutes, announce: *Please stop now.*

Stop music. Make the following announcement:

*Between this session and the next, review the list of optional activities. Do as many of them as you want to.*

_____, *will you please read aloud Preparation for the Next Session on page 125?*

After the section is read, thank the reader and give the following instructions:

*We will finish with our closing song, "I Love Myself," by Jai Josefs. The words are on page 40 of your workbook. Please help put the room back in order before you leave.*

*Now, form a circle, join hands, and sing together.*

Play the song on the tape player and sing along. When the song is over, announce:

*Thank you for coming. Our next meeting will be at* _____ (place), *at* _____ (time and day). *See you next time.*

*Timekeeper's*
*Guide For*

SESSION 13

# PARENTING YOUR
# OWN INNER CHILD

Be sure you have reviewed the information in General Guidelines for the Timekeeper: Sessions 3-14.

Before the meeting, be sure you have the necessary materials:

- Nametags
- Two tapes of background music
- One tape of "The Greatest Love of All"
- One tape of "I Love Myself"
- A timer
- A tape player (be sure you know how to use it)

Arrange the chairs in circles of six facing each other.

Reward promptness by beginning the meeting on time.

*Welcome to the thirteenth session of Parenting Each Other. My name is* _____, *and I'm your Timekeeper for this session, Parenting Your Own Inner Child.*

Ask the first reader: _____, *will you please read the commitment statements on page 23?*

209

After the section is read, thank the reader and ask the next reader: _____
_____, *will you please read the*
*Agreements to Create Safety, Trust, and Consistency, on pages 28-29?*

After the section is read, thank the reader and give the following instructions:

*We will start this session with a brief time for sharing. During this time you may share anything at all with other members of your small group. Remember that there are six people in your small group and only 10 minutes for sharing, so please be concise.*

*The first person to share will be the person closest to me. You will start by saying, "What I feel like saying is . . ." and complete a sentence or two about anything important to you right now. When you are finished, turn to the person on your right and say, ". . . and that's what I feel like saying. What do you feel like saying, (Jim, Mary, etc.)?" The next person then says, "What I feel like saying is . . ." Keep going around the group until I tell you it's time to stop. If you have nothing to share, say, "I pass."*

*You will have 10 minutes to share. I will give you a warning two minutes before the time is complete. Start now.*

Begin music faintly in the background. Announce the two-minute warning after eight minutes, and say *Please stop now,* at 10 minutes.

Stop music. Read the introduction to Parenting Your Own Inner Child on page 127. Ask the next reader:
_____, *will you please read the*
*introduction to the Self-Assessment Questionnaire, on page 128?* After the section is read, thank the reader and give the following instructions:

*Please take seven minutes to complete this new Self-Assessment Questionnaire.*

Start music. Allow seven minutes. Announce when the time is up. Then give the following instructions:

*Please take 10 minutes to complete Worksheet #18: Caring for Your Inner Child, on pages 130-131.*

At five minutes, announce, *Half the time is up.* At eight minutes announce, *You have two minutes left.* At 10 minutes, announce, *Please stop now.*

Stop music. Then give the following instructions:

*The instructions for the exercise are on page 131. Let each person in your small group take up to one minute to share their own insights gained from filling out the Worksheet. Each of you will have time to describe one incident and the changes you have made in self-nurturing. You'll have a total of 15 minutes for this part of the exercise. Discuss as many questions as you have time for. Don't worry if you don't answer them all. Be sure to acknowledge each other for the changes you've been making. Start now.*

Start music. At seven minutes, say, *Half the time is up.* At 13 minutes, say, *You have two minutes left.* At 15 minutes, say, *Please stop now.*

Have all participants take a 10-minute break. At 10 minutes, stop the music and ask participants to form a large circle.

Read the introduction to the Centering Ritual on page 131. Play the tape of "The Greatest Love of All" loudly. Stop the tape promptly when the song is over.

Have the participants return to their small group area. When they are settled, read the introductory paragraphs of the visualization on page 132 and give the following instructions:

*Now, prepare to parent your own Inner Child. Sit quietly with nothing in your lap and follow along with the visualization.*

Play the tape recording of the visualization or, if you are reading it, play quiet music in the background as you read. Read Slowly! When you have finished reading the visualization, give the following instructions:

*Take five minutes to write about your experience.* Start music. After five minutes say, *Please stop now.*

*You will have 30 minutes to discuss, in your small group, the answers to the questions on page 134. I will tell you when 15 minutes and 25 minutes have passed, and when to stop.*

Start music. Announce times at 15 minutes and 25 minutes. At 30 minutes, stop the discussion and announce:

*Please take a five-minute break, then return to your small group and complete Worksheet #19: Emotions — Windows To Your Past, on pages 134-135.*

*Take about five minutes to work on the Worksheet. When that is complete, read the instructions for the Nurturing Exchange, on pages 135-136. We will start small group discussion of these instructions in 20 minutes.*

At 10 minutes, announce: *You have 10 minutes left.* At 15 minutes, announce a five-minute warning. At 20 minutes, say, *Please stop now.*

*Discuss and clarify the instructions and any reservations you may have in your small group. You will have five minutes for this discussion. If you need more time, please inform the Timekeeper.*

(Timekeeper: you have the option of giving the groups an additional five minutes at this point.) Announce when time is up. Give the following instructions:

*Now, choose a partner. Decide which role you will take and proceed with the exchange. I'll give a two-minute warning, and I'll tell you when to stop. Begin now.*

At eight minutes, announce the two-minute warning. At 10 minutes, announce: *Please stop now. Find your workbook and write about your experience for two or three minutes. When you've finished writing, share your experience with your partner. In seven minutes we will choose new partners and repeat the exercise. Begin writing now.*

At three minutes, announce: *Please share with your partner now.* At seven minutes, announce:

*Please stop. Now, choose a new partner who had the opposite role from yours. You will change roles. Review the instructions for your new role. We will start the new Nurturing Exchange in five minutes.*

At five minutes say, *Please begin the Nurturing Exchange. I will tell you when the time is up, as I did before.* Give the two-minute warning at eight minutes. At 10 minutes say, *Please stop now. Find your workbook. Write briefly about your experience and share your experience with your partner. You will have seven minutes to write and share.*

At three minutes announce: *Please begin to share with your partner now.* At seven minutes, announce: *Please stop now.*

Stop music. Make the following announcement:

*Between this session and the next, review the list of optional activities. Do as many of them as you want to.*

_____, *will you please read aloud Preparation for the Next Session on page 138?*

After the section is read, thank the reader and give the following instructions:

*We will finish with our closing song, "I Love Myself," by Jai Josefs. The words are on page 40 of your workbook. Please help put the room back in order before you leave.*

*Now, form a circle, join hands, and sing together.*

Play the song on the tape player and sing along. When the song is over, announce:

*Thank you for coming. Our next meeting will be at* _____ (place), *at* _____ (time and day). *See you next time.*

*Timekeeper's*
*Guide For*

SESSION 14

# LEAVING
# HOME

Be sure you have reviewed the information in General Guidelines for the Timekeeper: Sessions 3-14.

Before the meeting, be sure you have the necessary materials:

- Nametags
- Two tapes of background music
- One tape of "The Greatest Love of All"
- One tape of "I Love Myself"
- A timer
- A tape player (be sure you know how to use it)
- Magic markers or crayons
- Large sheets of newsprint — at least one for each participant
- Masking tape to fasten the newsprint to the participants

Arrange the chairs in circles of six facing each other.

Reward promptness by beginning the meeting on time.

*Welcome to the fourteenth and last session of Parenting Each Other. My name is _____, and I'm your Timekeeper for this session, Leaving Home.*

213

Ask the first reader: _____, *will you please read the commitment statements on page 23?*

After the section is read, thank the reader and ask the next reader: _____, *will you please read the Agreements To Create Safety, Trust And Consistency on pages 28-29?*

After the section is read, thank the reader and give the following instructions:

*We will start this session with a brief time for sharing. During this time you may share anything at all with other members of your small group. Remember that there are six people in your small group and only 10 minutes for sharing, so please be concise.*

*The first person to share will be the person closest to me. You will start by saying, "What I feel like saying is . . ." and complete a sentence or two about anything important to you right now. When you are finished, turn to the person on your right and say, ". . . and that's what I feel like saying. What do you feel like saying, (Jim, Mary, etc.)?" The next person then says, "What I feel like saying is . . ." Keep going around the group until I tell you it's time to stop. If you have nothing to share, say, "I pass."*

*You will have 10 minutes to share. I will give you a warning two minutes before the time is complete. Start now.*

Begin music faintly in the background. Announce the two-minute warning after eight minutes, and say *Please stop now* at 10 minutes.

Stop music. Read the introduction to Leaving Home on page 139. Then give the following instructions:

*Please review the Self-Assessment Questionnaire that you completed in the last session. Make note of the developmental areas where your Inner Child is still looking for additional parenting. You will use this information later in the session. You'll have five minutes for this activity. Begin now.*

Start music. At three minutes, say, *You have two minutes left.* At five minutes, say, *Please stop now.* Give the following instructions:

*Please take eight minutes to complete Worksheet #20: Your Personal Network, on pages 141-142.*

At six minutes, announce, *You have two minutes left.* At eight minutes, announce, *Please stop.*

Stop music. Then give the following instructions:

*The instructions for the exercise are on page 142. Let each person in your small group take up to one minute to share their own insights gained from filling out the Worksheet. Then discuss the questions that are in your workbook. You'll have 10 minutes for this part of the exercise. Discuss as many questions as you have time for. Don't worry if you don't answer them all. Start now.*

Start music. At five minutes, say *The time is half up.* At eight minutes, say *You have two minutes left.* At 10 minutes, say, *Please stop now.*

Have all participants take a 10-minute break. At 10 minutes, stop the music and ask participants to form a large circle.

Read the introduction to the Centering Ritual on page 142. Play the tape of "The Greatest Love of All" loudly. Stop the tape promptly when the song is over.

Have the participants return to their small group area. When people are settled, read the introductory paragraphs of the visualization on page 142, then give the following instructions:

*Sit quietly with nothing in your lap and follow along with the last visualization of this program.*

Play the tape recording of the visualization or, if you are reading it, play quiet music in the background as you read. Read Slowly! When you have finished the visualization, give the following instructions:

*Take five minutes to write about your experience. When you've completed writing, please take five additional minutes to complete Worksheet #21: Your Future, on pages 144-145.*

Start music. At five minutes, say, *Start your Worksheet now.* At eight minutes, give a two-minute warning. At 10 minutes, say, *Please stop now.*

*In your small group, first, share the important parts of your visualization. Then focus on the course of your life after you've completed the recovery process. Take 15 minutes to complete your discussion.*

At seven minutes, say, *Half the time is up.* At 13 minutes, announce a two-minute warning. At 15 minutes, say, *Please stop now.*

*Take a five-minute break. Then return to your small group and read the information about Future Nurturing Exchanges, on pages 145-146. We will start the small group discussion of this information in 12 minutes.*

After 12 minutes have passed, announce: *Discuss and clarify the information about Future Nurturing Exchanges in your small group for the next 10 minutes.*

At five minutes, announce that five minutes are left. At eight mintues, give a two-minute warning. At 10 minutes, say, *Please stop now.* Stop music.

Decide on locations within the room for four different groups of people. Then announce: *People who want to exchange nurturing activities with other people in the program, please go to* (a place you designate). *People who want to create an advanced nurturing exchange group using the suggested guidelines, please go to* (a place you designate). *People who want to repeat this program and invite new people to join, please go to* (a place you designate). *People who plan to ask for nurturing from people in your existing support system, please go to* (a place you designate).

*In your discussion groups, review the instructions that are appropriate to accomplish your goals. You will have 15 minutes to complete this activity.*

Start music. At seven minutes, say, *Half your time is up.* Give a two-minute warning at 13 minutes. At 15 minutes, say, *Please stop now.*

Give each person a large, blank, sheet of newsprint, preferably at least 11" x 17". Then give the following instructions:

*Take this paper and tape it on your back. Take a crayon or light marker pen and move around the room. Write any positive comments you want to on others' papers, while the papers are on their backs. Write on the papers of as many different people as you can during the next few minutes.*

Allow the exercise to go on for 5 to 10 minutes, depending upon the size and activity of the group. Give a two-minute warning before you stop. At the end of the time you have allotted, say, *Please stop now.*

*Take the paper off your back, and read it. These are the strokes that other people in the group are giving you. Now, in your small group, stand up and read aloud all of the strokes you have received. After each person is finished, applaud and move on to the next person.*

If the entire group is fewer than 16 people, have each person read their strokes to the entire group. When the process is complete, give the following instructions:

*We will finish with our closing song, "I Love Myself," by Jai Josefs. The words are on page 40 of your workbook. Please help put the room back in order before you leave.*

*Now, form a circle, join hands, and sing together.*

Play the song. *Have a good life.*

# REFERENCES

Adams, R., **Watership Down,** (New York, NY: Avon), 1975.

Clark, J., & Dawson, C., **Growing Up Again: Parenting Ourselves, Parenting Our Children,** (New York, NY: Hazelden/Harper & Row), 1989.

Clarke, J., **Self-Esteem: A Family Affair,** (Minneapolis, MN: Winston Press), 1978.

Fisher, R., and Urey, W., **Getting To Yes: Negotiating Agreement Without Giving In,** (Boston, MA: Houghton Mifflin), 1981.

Freiberg, S., **The Magic Years,** (New York, NY: Charles Scribner's Sons), 1959.

**Gates Of Repentance: The New Union Prayer Book For The Days Of Awe,** (New York, NY: Central Conference of American Rabbis), 1978.

Gordon, T., **Parent Effectiveness Training.** (New York, NY: Peter H. Wyden, Inc.), 1970.

Levin, P., **Becoming The Way We Are: A Transactional Guide To Personal Development,** (Deerfield Beach, FL: Health Communications, Inc.), 1989.

Levin, P., **Cycles Of Power: A Guidebook To The Stages Of Life,** (Deerfield Beach, FL: Health Communications, Inc.), 1989.

Melody, P., et al., **Facing Co-dependence,** (New York, NY: Harper & Row), 1989.

Sher, B., **Wishcraft,** (New York, NY: Random House), 1979.

Weiss, L., & Weiss, J., **Recovery From Co-dependency: It's Never Too Late To Reclaim Your Childhood,** (Deerfield Beach, FL: Health Communications, Inc.), 1989.

# BIBLIOGRAPHY
## (Children's Books)

Aitken, Amy, **Ruby The Red Knight**, (Scarsdale, NY: Bradbury Press), 1983.

Alexander, Lloyd, **The King's Fountain**, (New York, NY: Dutton), 1971.

Allard, Harry, **It's So Nice To Have A Wolf Around The House**, (Garden City, NY: Doubleday), 1977.

Anderson, Eloise A., **Carlos Goes To School**, (New York, NY: F. Warne), 1973.

Anno, Mitsumas, **The King's Flower**, (New York, NY: Collins), 1976.

Atwater, Richard, **Mr. Popper's Penguins**, (Boston, MA: Little, Brown), 1966.

Babbitt, Natalie, **The Something**, (New York, NY: Farrar, Straus & Giroux), 1970.

**Babies First Book**, Platt & Munk Teddy Board Books, (New York, NY: Putnam Publishing Group), 1978.

**Baby Animals**, Platt & Munk Teddy Board Books, (New York, NY: Putnam Publishing Group), 1978.

Baylor, Byrd, **Sometimes I Dance Mountains**, (New York, NY: Scribner), 1973.

Bemelmans, Ludwig, **Madeline And The Bad Hat**, (New York, NY: Puffin Books), 1956.

Berenstain, Stan and Jan, **Bears In The Night**, (New York, NY: Random House), 1971.

Blume, Judy, **Iggie's House**, (Englewood Cliffs, NJ: Bradbury Press), 1970.

Bond, Michael, **Paddington's Garden**, (New York, NY: Random House), 1972.

Butterworth, Nick, **Nice Or Nasty: A Book Of Opposites**, (Boston, MA: Little, Brown), 1987.

Carle, Eric, **Very Hungry Caterpillar,** (New York, NY: Philomel Books), 1979.

Cleary, Beverly, **Beezus And Ramona** (New York, NY: Dell), 1955.

_____, **The Mouse And The Motorcycle,** (New York, NY: Morrow), 1965.

_____, **Ramona The Brave,** (New York, NY: Morrow), 1975.

Collier, James Lincoln, **Rock Star,** (New York, NY: Simon & Schuster), 1988.

Colman, Hila, **Chicano Girl,** (New York, NY: Morrow), 1973.

Dahl, Roald, **Charlie And The Chocolate Factory,** (New York, NY: Knopf), 1964.

Dana, Barbara, **Necessary Parties,** (New York, NY: Bantam Books), 1986.

Danziger, Paula, **Can You Sue Your Parents For Malpractice?,** (New York, NY: Dell), 1979.

_____, **The Pistachio Prescription,** (New York, NY: Delacorte Press), 1978.

_____, **There's A Bat In Bunk Five,** (New York, NY: Dell), 1980.

Davidson, Margaret, **Helen Keller,** (New York, NY: Hastings House), 1969.

_____, **Louis Braille: The Boy Who Invented Books For The Blind,** (New York, NY: Hastings House), 1971.

Eastman, P.D., **Are You My Mother?,** (New York, NY: Beginner Books), 1960.

Ford, George, **Babies First Picture Book,** (New York, NY: Random House), 1979.

Freed, Alvyn M., **TA For Tots, Volume I And II,** (Sacramento, CA: Jalmar Press), 1971.

Freeman, Don, **Corduroy,** (New York, NY: Viking Press), 1968.

Gwynne, Fred, **The King Who Rained,** (New York, NY: Windmill/Simon & Schuster), 1970.

Hazen, Barbara Shook, **Even If I Did Something Awful,** (New York, NY: Atheneum), 1981.

Henderson, Kathy, **Babies Book Of Babies,** (New York, NY: Dial Books for Young Readers), 1988.

Hughes, Shirley, **Alfie Gets In First,** (New York, NY: Mulberry Books), 1981.

_____, **David And Dog,** (Englewood Cliffs, NJ: Prentice-Hall), 1977.

Johnson, John E., **The Me Book,** (New York, NY: Random House), 1979.

Juster, Norton, **The Phantom Tollbooth,** (New York, NY: Random House), 1961.

Klein, Norma, **Mom, The Wolfman, And Me,** (New York, NY: Avon Books), 1972.

Konigsburg, E.L., **From The Mixed-Up Files Of Mrs. Basil E. Frankweiler,** (New York, NY: Dell), 1967.

Kunhardt, Dorothy, **Pat The Bunny,** (Racine, WI: Golden Press, Western Publishing), n.d.

Lamorisse, A., **The Red Balloon,** (Garden City, NY: Doubleday), 1957.

Lawson, Robert, **Ben And Me,** (Boston, MA: Little, Brown), 1939.

Leaf, Munro, **The Story Of Ferdinand,** (Harmonsworth, MX: Penguin Books), 1964.

LeSieg, Theo, **Ten Apples Up On Top,** (New York, NY: Beginner Books), 1961.

_____, **I Wish That I Had Duck Feet,** (New York, NY: Beginner Books), 1965.

Lindgren, Astrid, **Pippi Longstocking,** (Oxford: Windrush), 1979.

Lionni, Leo, **Fish Is Fish,** (New York, NY: Pantheon Books), 1970.

Lipkind, William and Mordvinoff, Nicolas, **Finders Keepers,** (New York, NY: Harcourt, Brace), 1951.

Lowry, Lois, **A Summer To Die,** (Toronto, New York: Bantam Books), 1977.

McCloskey, Robert, **Make Way For Ducklings,** (New York, NY: Viking), 1941.

MacDonald, Betty, **Mrs. Piggle Wiggle,** (Philadelphia, PA: Lippincott), 1947.

Mayer, Mercer, **There's A Nightmare In My Closet,** (New York, NY: Dial Press), 1968.

Mayle, Peter, **Where Did I Come From?,** (Seacaucus, NJ: L. Stuart), 1973.

Miklowitz, Gloria, **The Day The Senior Class Got Married,** (New York, NY: Dell), 1983.

Milne, A.A., **Winnie The Pooh,** (New York, NY: Dutton), 1954.

O'Dell, Scott, **Island Of Blue Dolphins,** (Santa Barbara, CA: Cornerstone Books), 1960.

Parish, Peggy, **Amelia Bedelia,** (New York, NY: Harper), 1963.

Paterson, Katherine, **Jacob Have I Loved,** (New York, NY: Avon Books), 1980.

Peet, Bill, **Eli,** (Boston, MA: Houghton, Mifflin), 1978.

Piper, Walter, **The Little Engine That Could,** (New York, NY: Platt & Munk), 1976.

Ravilious, Robin, **The Runaway Chick,** (New York, NY: Macmillan), 1987.

Reys, Margret and H.A., **Curious George Goes Hiking,** (Boston, MA: Houghton Mifflin), 1985.

Robins, Joan, **My Brother, Will,** (New York, NY: Greenwillow Books), 1986.

Ross, Katharine, **When You Were A Baby,** (New York, NY: Random House), 1988.

Schwartz, Alvin, **A Twister Of Twists, A Tangler Of Tongues,** (New York, NY: Harper & Row), 1972.

Sendak, Maurice, **Where The Wild Things Are,** (New York, NY: Harper and Row), 1963.

Seuss, T.G., **Cat In The Hat,** (New York, NY: Random House), 1957.

_____, **Dr. Seuss's ABC,** (New York, NY: Beginner Books), 1963.

_____, **Fox In Socks,** (New York, NY: Beginner Books), 1965.

_____, **Green Eggs And Ham,** (Westminster, MD: Random House/Miller-Brody), 1976.

_____, **Hunches In Bunches,** (New York, NY: Random House), 1982.

_____, **McElligot's Pool,** (New York, NY: Random House), 1947.

_____, **One Fish, Two Fish, Red Fish, Blue Fish,** (New York, NY: Beginner Books; Distributed by Random House), 1960.

_____, **The Lorax,** (New York, NY: Random House), 1971.

_____, **Yertle The Turtle,** (New York, NY: Random House), 1958.

Sharmat, Marjorie Wienman, **A Big, Fat, Enormous Lie,** (New York, NY: Dutton), 1978.

_____, **I'm Terrific,** (New York, NY: Holiday House), 1977.

Smith, Lucia B., **A Special Kind Of Sister,** (New York, NY: Holt, Rinehart, & Winston), 1979.

Sutton, Eve, **My Cat Likes To Hide In Boxes,** (New York, NY: Parents' Magazine Press), 1974.

Thomson, Julian F., **Grounding Of Group Six,** (New York, NY: Avon Books), 1983.

Udry, Janice May, **What Mary Jo Wanted**, (Chicago, IL: A. Whitman), 1968.

Vanhalewijn, Mariette, **Princess Penelope's 365 Dresses**, (New York, NY: 1970.

Ventura, Piero, **The Magic Well**, (New York, NY: Random House), 1976.

Viorst, Judith, **Alexander And The Terrible, Horrible, No Good, Very Bad Day**, (New York, NY: Atheneum), 1972.

_____, **My Mama Says There Aren't Any Zombies, Ghosts, Vampires, Creatures, Demons, Monsters, Fiends, Goblins Or Things**, (New York, NY: Atheneum), 1973.

Waber, Bernard, **Nobody Is Perfick**, (Boston, MA: Houghton Mifflin), 1971.

Waddell, Martin and Bensen, Patrick, **The Tough Princess**, (New York, NY: Philomel Books), 1987.

White, E.B., **Charlotte's Web**, (New York, NY: Harper Trophy Book), 1952.

Williams, Margery, **The Velveteen Rabbit**, New York, NY: (Knopf; Distributed by Random House), 1985.

Wilson, Sara, **Beware The Dragons**, (New York, NY: Harper & Row), 1985.

Zindel, Paul and Dragonwagon, Crescent, **To Take A Dare**, (New York, NY: Harper & Row), 1982.

Zolotow, Charlotte, **The Hating Book**, (New York, NY: Harper & Row), 1969.

_____, **William's Doll**, New York, NY: Harper & Row, 1972.

# Author's Note

I would appreciate your feedback about how this program is useful to you, how it could be improved and suggestions for further work in this area. Contact me at:

> Empowerment Systems
> 2275 East Arapahoe Road, Suite 306
> Littleton, Colorado 80122

For futher information about starting or locating a *Parenting Each Other* group call: (303) 794-5379.

# New Books . . .
## from Health Communications

*HEAL YOUR SELF-ESTEEM:* Recovery From Addictive Thinking
Bryan Robinson, Ph.D.

Do you have low self-esteem? Do you blame others for your own unhappiness? If so, you may be an addictive thinker. The 10 Principles For Healing, an innovative, positive approach to recovery, are integrated into this book to provide a new attitude with simple techniques for recovery.

ISBN 1-55874-119-4                                                     $9.95

*HEALING ENERGY:* The Power Of Recovery
Ruth Fishel, M.Ed., C.A.C.

Linking the newest medical discoveries in mind/body/spirit connections with the field of recovery, this book illustrates how to balance ourselves mentally, physically and spiritually to overcome our addictive behavior.

ISBN 1-55874-128-3                                                     $9.95

*CREDIT, CASH AND CO-DEPENDENCY:* The Money Connection
Yvonne Kaye, Ph.D.

Co-dependents and Adult Children seem to experience more problems than most as money can be used as an anesthetic or fantasy. Yvonne Kaye writes of the particular problems the co-dependent has with money, sharing her own experiences.

ISBN 1-55874-133-X                                                     $9.95

*THE LAUNDRY LIST:* The ACoA Experience
Tony A. and Dan F.

Potentially The Big Book of ACoA, *The Laundry List* includes stories, history and helpful information for the Adult Child of an alcoholic. Tony A. discusses what it means to be an ACoA and what the self-help group can do for its members.

ISBN 1-55874-105-4                                                     $9.95

*LEARNING TO SAY NO:* Establishing Healthy Boundaries
Carla Wills-Brandon, M.A.

If you grew up in a dysfunctional family, establishing boundaries is a difficult and risky decision. Where do you draw the line? Learn to recognize yourself as an individual who has the power to say no.

ISBN 1-55874-087-2                                                     $8.95

3201 S.W. 15th Street,
Deerfield Beach, FL 33442-8190
1-800-851-9100

Health
Communications, Inc.

# Other Books By . . .
## Health Communications

*ADULT CHILDREN OF ALCOHOLICS (Expanded)*
Janet Woititz
Over a year on *The New York Times* Best-Seller list, this book is the primer on Adult Children of Alcoholics.
**ISBN 1-55874-112-7**                                    **$8.95**

*STRUGGLE FOR INTIMACY*
Janet Woititz
Another best-seller, this book gives insightful advice on learning to love more fully.
**ISBN 0-932194-25-7**                                    **$6.95**

*BRADSHAW ON: THE FAMILY: A Revolutionary Way of Self-Discovery*
John Bradshaw
The host of the nationally televised series of the same name shows us how families can be healed and individuals can realize full potential.
**ISBN 0-932194-54-0**                                    **$9.95**

*HEALING THE SHAME THAT BINDS YOU*
John Bradshaw
This important book shows how toxic shame is the core problem in our compulsions and offers new techniques of recovery vital to all of us.
**ISBN 0-932194-86-9**                                    **$9.95**

*HEALING THE CHILD WITHIN: Discovery and Recovery for*
*Adult Children of Dysfunctional Families* — Charles Whitfield, M.D.
Dr. Whitfield defines, describes and discovers how we can reach our Child Within to heal and nurture our woundedness.
**ISBN 0-932194-40-0**                                    **$8.95**

*A GIFT TO MYSELF: A Personal Guide To Healing My Child Within*
Charles L. Whitfield, M.D.
Dr. Whitfield provides practical guidelines and methods to work through the pain and confusion of being an Adult Child of a dysfunctional family.
**ISBN 1-55874-042-2**                                    **$11.95**

*HEALING TOGETHER: A Guide To Intimacy And Recovery For*
*Co-dependent Couples* — Wayne Kritsberg, M.A.
This is a practical book that tells the reader why he or she gets into dysfunctional and painful relationships, and then gives a concrete course of action on how to move the relationship toward health.
**ISBN 1-55784-053-8**                                    **$8.95**

3201 S.W. 15th Street,
Deerfield Beach, FL 33442-8190
1-800-851-9100

Health Communications, Inc.